FROM THE
GAME TIME TALES
SERIES

STEPPING IN

THE JOURNEY

D.R.GORDON

Stepping In: The Journey
From the series - Game Time Tales
D. R. Gordon

For permission requests, contact the publisher at the address below.

D.R. Gordon
www.gametimetales.com

This book is available in print and digital formats and may be purchased through online retailers, including Amazon.com.

First Edition

ISBN: 978-1-7635073-0-2

Note: This book uses United States spelling and grammar conventions.

"For all my players that have come and gone"

Inspired by true events, this story stands as a testament to the belief that anything is possible if you are willing to work hard enough for it.

PROLOGUE

On the freshly polished floors of the Bayside Community Basketball Stadium, a place where basketball was played separate from the regular school teams, the Southside Strikers and Western Wolves, faced off in a display of youthful determination and raw talent. Among the flurry of ponytails and the chorus of squeaking sneakers, two players stood out, each a beacon of skill and competitive spirit on their respective teams.

For the Southside Strikers, there was Jordan, a dynamo of energy, toughness, and focus. Each time she had the ball, it seemed like the game shifted into a new gear. Her dribbles were purposeful, her eyes constantly scanning for an open teammate or a path to the basket. Her signature move was a swift crossover that left her defenders a step behind, followed by a gentle layup that kissed the glass before dropping through the net. Her presence on the court was an imposing mix of both a comfort to her team and a challenge to her opponents.

On the other side, wearing the colors of the Western Wolves, was Riley. With a competitive fire rarely matched, she was a force to be reckoned with. Riley's game was built on speed and agility. Her fast breaks were like lightning, her defensive steals a testament to her anticipation and quick reflexes. When she shot the ball, it was with a confidence that belied her years, each attempt a message that she was here to compete and compete to win.

The game was a back-and-forth affair, with Jordan and Riley often finding themselves in direct confrontation. Jordan would power through the defense, only to find Riley there, a steadfast obstacle. Riley would dart towards the basket, but Jordan's keen sense of the game often put her in the right position to challenge the shot. Their encounters were a captivating dance of skill and will, each movement and counter a testament to their dedication and love for the game.

As the game progressed, their individual brilliance not only highlighted their own abilities but also elevated the play of their teammates. Jordan's sharp passes and strategic playmaking created openings for the Strikers, while Riley's intensity and leadership rallied the Wolves, forging a unity that turned individual efforts into collective strength.

When the final whistle blew, it was clear that the score was just a number. Jordan, walking beside her coach with her game face still on, couldn't help but glance back at Riley. She whispered to her coach, a mix of admiration and challenge in her tone, "She's got game, coach. Next time, I'll be one step ahead."

Even as they walked away, Jordan's mind was racing, already plotting and planning for their next encounter on the court. It was clear that this was not just a game; it was the beginning of a rivalry that would push them both to their limits.

Riley, on the other side of the court, shared her own sentiments with her dad, her competitive spirit flaring. "Did you see how she plays? She's tough, but so am I," Riley said, her eyes sparkling with the challenge. "I won't let her win again. This is just the start, and I'm not backing down."

In those moments, with their families by their side, Jordan and Riley found not just the seeds of rivalry but also the drive to push themselves further. It was more than a game; it was the beginning of a journey, a duel of spirit and skill that would shape their paths in ways they couldn't yet imagine.

CHAPTER 1:

RILEY

Dear Basketball,

Today was the big game against Southside Strikers, and you know who, Jordan! She's super good at basketball - everyone says so. But you know what? I feel like I can be just as good, if not better!

The gym was like a jungle today, all loud and wild. We had to be fierce like lions on the court. Coach always talks about teamwork, and I get it, but deep down, isn't it also about proving yourself? Today, my heart pounded with the chance to show everyone, including myself, that I'm one of the best.

Jordan and I, we've had so many battles on the court. It's like we're in this big, thrilling adventure, always trying to outdo each other. But here's the crazy part - soon, we have tryouts for the Bayside Waves. We might end up playing together! How amazing would that be? It's like my two favorite worlds colliding – competing and maybe even teaming up with Jordan.

I'm lying here in my bed, the moonlight streaming through the window, and I can't help but feel a bundle of nerves. What if Coach doesn't pick me? What if I trip up or miss an important shot? But then, I imagine Jordan and me as this unstoppable duo on the court, and it's like a dream. It's the kind of excitement that feels like having your favorite ice cream and cake at the same time!

As I scribble these thoughts down, I remind myself that tomorrow's a new day, a new game. I'll put on my best game face, and show them all how awesome Riley is. And who knows, maybe this is where Jordan and I start an epic journey together in this big basketball adventure!

Until next time,

Riley

CHAPTER 2:

RILEY'S FIRST STEP

Riley Mitchell, a whirlwind of energy and confidence, lived for two things: her family and basketball. Nestled in the heart of a bustling neighborhood, Riley's room screamed of her twin passions. Posters of basketball legends adorned the walls, and her collection of basketballs sat proudly in the corner.

Every day after school, Riley would rush home, backpack swinging, and basketball in hand. She'd trade her school shoes for sneakers faster than you could say "slam dunk" and head straight to the basketball ring in her backyard.

"Riley, homework first!" her Mum would call, but Riley had a different agenda. Basketball was her homework, her classroom, and her favorite subject. She practiced her ninja-like moves, weaving around imaginary defenders, and shooting with the precision of a seasoned pro. As she swooped across the court, effortlessly snatching the ball from her opponent's grasp, a cheer erupted from the sidelines.

"She's on fire!" Riley would think to herself.
Her parents, watching from the kitchen window, were full of support towards her basketball. Her father, apron-clad busy with the evening's meal and occasionally glancing out, would say with pride, "She gets better every day." Her mother, busy at work on her laptop grading her student's work, would smile in agreement adding, "And she's still acing her studies. She's our little superstar."

Every week, Riley played in the local competition for her team, the Western Wolves. The other players and spectators knew something Riley only dared to believe: she wasn't just good, she was exceptional. One of the best in the whole league!

"Mum, Dad, watch this!" Riley would call, attempting a daring shot. The ball arced high, sailing over the flowerbeds – a perfect shot. "And she scores!" her dad would announce, mimicking a sports commentator with his deep loud voice, and proudly signaling 3 points with his hand, as the ball swished through the net.

As the sun dipped below the horizon, signaling the end of another day, Riley lay on the grass, her thoughts drifting to the tryouts. Tomorrow was not just another day – it was the doorway to her dreams. She retreated to her room, her heart filled with a mix of excitement and anxiety, dreaming of making it big on the basketball court.

As the evening approached, and the stars began to twinkle outside Riley's window, the excitement in her chest grew. The next day was the tryouts for the Bayside Waves, the representative team of the entire local competition. Riley couldn't shake the thrill that came with the possibility of becoming a basketball star. She wondered if she was ever going to be able to fall asleep tonight. Eventually, she drifted off, dreaming of fast breaks, swished shots, and the journey that basketball could one day take her on.

The next day dawned with an air of anticipation. Riley, in her favorite basketball jersey, practically skipped to the local sports center. The buzz of excitement enveloped her as she entered the gym, the familiar scent of polished wood and the rhythmic dribbling of basketballs setting the stage for potential greatness.
Coach Ethan, clipboard in hand, greeted each hopeful player with a nod. Riley had seen Coach Ethan around the courts, but never really met him before. The room echoed with the squeaks of sneakers and the bouncing basketballs. Riley took her place on the

court, her stomach aflutter of butterflies ready to escape but she was ready, determined to showcase the skills she had honed in her backyard. Her eyes scanned the gym, recognising many girls from the local league.

The local competition was a gateway to something bigger. Each suburb had its own team, competing fiercely in the local league. The best players from each local team were invited to try out for the representative squad competing against teams from different zones across the entire state.

Her mind flashed back to when she and Jordan, faced off in a local league game not that long ago. Riley's team, the Western Wolves, and Jordan's team, the Southside Strikers, clashed in a memorable battle. It was a game that echoed with the cheers of proud parents and the laughter of determined young players.

In the midst of that game, even at such a young age, Riley and Jordan displayed the spark that would define their future battles on the court. The Wolves and Strikers, two teams destined to cross paths again and again, had no idea that in just a few months, the two girls would stand on the same court, vying for a spot in the representative squad of the Bayside Waves.

As Riley scanned the crowd, there, among the sea of aspiring players, she spotted Jordan. Their eyes met, a silent acknowledgment of the journey that had brought them to this moment. Riley's heart raced as the tryouts commenced, her mind a whirlwind of excitement intertwined with nerves. Doubts flickered through her thoughts, whispering fears of not being good enough or missing the cut for the team. Yet, despite the stubborn shadow of self-doubt, she stood ready to give her all, her resolve unwavering in the face of uncertainty.

CHAPTER 3:

JORDAN

Dear Basketball,

Today was super tough. We played against the Western Wolves, and this girl called Riley, and we didn't win. My hand is kinda shaky writing this because losing is really hard.

The gym was so loud with the Wolves cheering. Our side was pretty quiet. After the game, Coach told us, "Remember, it's all about loving the game." I know he's right, but losing still feels bad.

I saw Riley after the game. She won, but she wasn't bragging or anything. We looked at each other, and I kinda nodded. It's funny – she's on the other team, but I think she's pretty cool. We both just really love basketball. But I really want to win next time.

Leaving the gym, I kept thinking about one part of the game. I was close to scoring, but then I slipped, and Riley got the ball. The sound of the other team cheering keeps playing in my head.

But diary, this isn't the end for me. It's just one bad day. I'm going to use this to get better. My team, the Southside Strikers, needs me. I'm going to practice more and get stronger.

I can't wait until we play the Wolves again. Next time, we'll be the ones cheering. I'm going to work hard, practice my shots, and just get better every day.

Until next time, it's all about bouncing back, aiming high, and dreaming about all the fun games ahead.

Jordan

CHAPTER 4:

JORDAN'S PATH TO THE TRYOUTS

In the evening, after a busy day at school, Jordan Buchanan and her teammates from the Southside Strikers gathered for practice.The air was alive with the rhythmic sound of basketballs against the pavement and the spirited chatter of her team. They were united by their love for the game and their determination to excel at the upcoming Bayside Waves tryouts.

Jordan dribbled the ball with a practiced ease, weaving through her teammates in a mock drill. "Nice move, Jordan!" called out Mia, one of her closest teammates. Jordan flashed a grin, feeling a surge of pride. These moments of camaraderie and challenge were what she lived for.

As they practiced, Jordan's mind occasionally drifted back to their recent game against the Western Wolves. The loss stung, but Coach's words echoed in her ears: "It's the tough games that teach us the most." She knew she was right. Every pass, every drill, and every shot were steps towards becoming better.

With each day, the tryouts for the Waves loomed larger. Jordan pushed herself harder, her determination unwavering. She became a pillar of support for her team, cheering them on, laughing off mishaps, and celebrating every small victory. For Jordan, the court was more than just a place to play; it was where her competitive fire could be unleashed.

As the tryouts approached, a mix of excitement and butterflies filled Jordan. She thought about the players from the Wolves, especially Riley, whose skill she admired from afar. There was a part of her that wanted ever so badly to prove that she was the better player, but there was also a thought, a quiet wish, to play alongside Riley, to see what they could achieve together on the court.

In the evenings, the backyard hoop became Jordan's sanctuary. The cool night air brushed against her skin as she practiced shot after shot, the hoop a silent companion in the dimming light. Each throw wasn't just about accuracy; it was about preparing mentally, visualizing success, and overcoming nerves.

The day of the tryouts dawned bright and clear. Jordan's heart was a drumbeat of anticipation as she laced up her sneakers. She took a deep, steadying breath, reminding herself why she played – for the love of the game, for the journey, for the friendships.

Stepping onto the court, the sounds of the game enveloped her – the squeak of sneakers, the thud of basketballs, the murmurs of eager players. Her eyes scanned the crowd, and there was Riley, a familiar face amidst the sea of hopefuls. Their eyes met, a silent exchange of respect and understanding. The moment was brief but significant, a recognition of their shared passion and the new chapter that was about to unfold.

CHAPTER 5:

THE TRYOUTS

The stadium was a hive of activity, buzzing with the rhythmic bounce of basketballs and the hum of eager conversation. Riley and Jordan stood at opposing ends of the court, their glances conveying a mutual understanding and shared excitement for the challenge ahead.

With a clipboard in hand, Coach Ethan surveyed the eager assembly of hopefuls, his experienced gaze discerning potential amid the sea of faces. Familiar with the rhythms of many seasons past, he felt a blend of nerves and excitement stir within him at the prospect of sculpting a new team, each player a fresh story waiting to unfold on his court. As he called for attention, a hush fell over the gym, every player poised for the first trial of their skills.

The dribbling duel was the first spectacle. Riley's crossovers were fluid and graceful, a dance that would leave her defenders trailing. She could feel the court beneath her feet, the smoothness of the ball in her hands. Across from her, Jordan displayed a different kind of mastery – explosive bursts, her powerful dribbles echoing in the gym as a statement of her presence.

Next came the passing drills. Riley's passes were sharp and intuitive, each one finding Jordan as if magnetically drawn. Jordan, in turn, delivered the ball with a mix of power and precision, each pass setting Riley up for stunning finishes. The onlookers couldn't help but gasp at the duo's seamless coordination. Coach Ethan glanced at his clipboard, then back at the court, his thoughts clear. With such seamless teamwork and synchronicity on display, it seemed undeniable—these two must have been playing together for quite some time. But this was not the case.

During the defensive drills, their versatility shone through. Jordan's movements were like a controlled storm, disrupting plays with fierce determination. Riley, with her quick reflexes, seemed to anticipate her opponent's moves, intercepting passes with an almost telepathic precision.

In a particularly memorable play, Riley's quick hands snatched the ball, swiftly passing to Jordan. Drawing the defense towards her, Jordan lobbed a perfect pass back to Riley, who landed a mid-range shot with ease. Coach Ethan, watching from the sidelines, nodded in approval, sensing the potential in their synergy.

Maya, a well-known sharpshooter in the local league, stepped up, ready to showcase her skill. As she positioned herself for her signature shot, Riley, with cat-like agility, intercepted the ball and wove through the defenders. With a quick flick of the wrist, she passed to Jordan, who finished the play with an impressive fast-break.

As the final buzzer echoed through the gym, the girls gathered, their hearts pounding. The tryouts had been a testament to the players' hard work and dedication. Coach Ethan, a small smile playing on his lips, gathered the girls. "You've all shown great heart today. I'm proud to announce the new lineup for the Bayside Waves."

A ripple of anticipation passed through the players as Coach Ethan read out the names. Riley and Jordan shared a look of quiet triumph as their names were called, a silent acknowledgment of their journey and the new chapter that lay ahead.

After the announcement, Maya approached Riley and Jordan, her excitement palpable. "You two were amazing out there! I can't wait to see what we can all achieve together," she exclaimed, her words echoing the sentiments of the forming team.

Alex, known for her strategic play, nodded in agreement. "Your teamwork really stood out today. It's going to be an exciting season."

The conversation soon turned to shared experiences, favorite moments from past games, and tips for improvement. Riley and Jordan found themselves at the heart of these exchanges, feeling an authentic sense of belonging and excitement for the season ahead.

As the gym doors closed behind them, the echoes of the day's trials faded into the night. In the backseat of Riley's car, her parents exchanged proud glances. "So, Riley, how did it go?" her dad asked with a knowing smile.

Riley's face lit up with joy. "It was incredible, Dad! Jordan was there, and we just clicked. It's like we've been playing together for years!"

Her mum, sharing in the excitement, added, "That's fantastic, honey. I'm so proud of you."

Meanwhile, in Jordan's car, a similar scene unfolded. Her dad peeked at her in the rearview mirror, his eyes sparkling with curiosity. "So, Jordan, how was it?"

Jordan's grin was wide and genuine. "Dad, it was amazing! Riley was there, and we were unstoppable together. It's like we're meant to be on the same team."

Her mum, beaming with pride, chimed in, "That's wonderful, Jordan! I can't wait to see you two in action!"

As the two cars made their way through the quiet streets, Riley and Jordan, in their respective worlds, shared their excitement and dreams for the season ahead. Unbeknownst to each other, their feelings of joy and anticipation were mirrored, setting the stage for a remarkable partnership on the court.

CHAPTER 6:

A DYNAMIC DEBUT

In the days leading up to the Bayside Waves' first game, excitement and anticipation were palpable. On the practice court, Riley and Jordan worked tirelessly under Coach Ethan's watchful eye. As the first official training session of the new Bayside Waves team commenced, Coach Ethan, a figure of authority and encouragement, gathered the team at center court.

"Alright, team, let's start strong and build our foundation," Coach Ethan announced. "We'll focus on fundamental skills today, ensuring we're all on the same page."

The session kicked off with basic dribbling drills. Each player was tasked with maneuvering through a series of cones, ensuring they kept their heads up and eyes forward, promoting court awareness and ball control. Riley, with her smooth ball-handling ability, felt right at home. The sound of basketballs pattered in a steady beat, a testament to the focus and determination of each player.

Next, they transitioned to passing drills. Players paired up and practiced chest passes, bounce passes, and, much to the delight of Jordan, the no-look pass, emphasizing accuracy and the importance of communication. "Anticipate your teammate's movements, and make sure your passes are crisp and direct," Coach Ethan instructed, observing the pairs weave their synergy and precision into every pass.

Next on the agenda were shooting drills. The players formed orderly lines around the key, each taking their turn to practice free throws and jump shots off the dribble and catch and shoot from a pass. Coach Ethan paced alongside them, offering guidance. "Keep your focus sharp, maintain your form, and follow through," he advised. "Remember, consistency and rhythm are your best allies." Amidst the repetitive swish of the net, Riley's attention was drawn to Maya's impeccable shooting form, a mental note etching itself into her mind for future matchups.

As the session progressed, they incorporated defensive drills, practicing footwork, and learning how to maintain a solid defensive stance. "Defense is about effort and attitude," Coach Ethan asserted. "Stay alert, keep your feet moving, and always be ready to react." Jordan couldn't help but notice how agile Alex was on her feet. Her timing and pressure were also of the highest order.

To wrap up the session, the team engaged in a scrimmage, applying the skills they honed into a game-like scenario. As Jess leaped and emphatically blocked a shot, Riley watched from the sidelines, giving an approving nod, impressed by her teammate's defensive prowess. It was an opportunity for the players to experience the flow of the game, to understand spacing and timing, and to bring together all the elements of basketball they'd practiced throughout the session.

As the final whistle blew, Coach Ethan gathered the team. "Great work today! Remember, every drill is a building block for our success. Let's keep this energy and focus going forward!"

The players left the court, fatigued but fulfilled, knowing that each drill, each piece of advice, and each moment spent on that court was a step towards becoming not just a team, but a force to be reckoned with.

Off the court, the team's bond strengthened. During a casual dinner, amidst pizza and laughter, the girls shared snippets of their lives. Riley and Jordan, though different, found common ground in their shared dreams and passion for the game. Maya joked about her love for late-night snacks, and Alex playfully recounted a clumsy moment during practice. Coach Ethan, more friend than coach in those moments, laughed with his new team helping lay the foundations for a strong bond between players and coach alike.

The night before the game, amidst the warmth of family dinners, Riley and Jordan drew strength from their loved ones. Riley's family reminisced about past games, their stories a tapestry of encouragement. Meanwhile, Jordan's younger brother's wide-eyed admiration for his sister's skill added a spark to her determination.

Game day arrived with a crisp autumn air, thick with promise. Riley and Jordan stepped onto the Waves' home court, their connection evident in their shared focus and determination. Seeing themselves in full uniform for the first time, a sense of pride and responsibility settled over them.

Coach Ethan's pre-game talk was a blend of strategy and motivation. "Today, we begin a journey," he said, his voice resonating with belief. "Trust in each other, and the game will take care of itself."

"Hands in," He said eagerly. "Waves on three" He continued.

As the countdown reached 3, The team excitedly yelled "Waves!"

As the jump ball for the first game of the season was thrown up, while the ball hung in the air all the nervous thoughts and uncertainty that Riley and Jordan had felt during the days leading up to the first game vanished. Jess, the team's center who was the tallest on the team and a great rebounder tipped the ball to Riley and in an instant, the girls' debut game was underway. Riley, with agile moves, broke through the defense and flicked the swiftest of passes to a slashing Jordan for the team's opening score of the season. A quick high five was shared, and without a thought, the girls were already into their defensive assignments.

Within what seemed like an instant, Jordan's defensive prowess shone as she stole the ball, executing a sleek behind-the-back pass to Riley that caught everyone off guard. The duo's synchronicity amplified the team's momentum, with Maya's sharp three-pointer and Alex's crucial steal adding to the excitement as the Waves jumped out to an early lead.

Coach Ethan, ever the tactician, guided the team through each play. His timeouts were not just strategic pauses but moments of encouragement, his advice weaving a stronger bond among the players.

As the game unfolded, Riley and Jordan's partnership blossomed, each play a testament to their growing understanding. Jess' rebounds and quick outlet passes complemented the duo's style, creating a fast-paced rhythm that was hard to counter.

When the final buzzer sounded, victory was theirs. The Waves' debut was marked by celebratory hugs and compliments between teammates and a high-five between Riley and Jordan, a symbol of their dynamic partnership. The cheers of proud parents and teammates filled the gym, a chorus of celebration for the promising season ahead.

Post-game, Coach Ethan's words echoed. "Today, you played as one. Remember, it's about growing together." Riley, Jordan, and the rest of the team left the court united, their spirits high and their bond stronger than ever.

In the post-game glow, Riley and Jordan shared a quiet moment of reflection. "We did it," Riley said, her eyes shining. Jordan nodded, a smile spreading across her face. "This is just the beginning."

CHAPTER 7:

2 STEPS FORWARD, 1 STEP BACK

In the soft glow of the setting sun, after she had finished her homework and dinner, Riley laced up her sneakers and stepped onto the familiar concrete of her backyard court. This was her sanctuary, a place where every dribble and every shot brought her closer to her dream.

With her basketball firmly in hand, Riley focused on perfecting her signature move, the one she felt in her bones every time she took to the court. She started with a steady dribble, feeling the rhythm of the ball tapping against the ground, a beat that matched the racing of her heart.

Then, with a swift and smooth motion, she executed her favorite maneuver: the behind-the-back dribble. It was a dance, a secret conversation between her and the ball. As she pulled off the move, she felt a surge of confidence, a silent whisper that said, "This is who you are."

But the move wasn't complete without the hesitation, that split-second pause that threw her imaginary defenders off balance. She relished the moment of stillness, the brief calm in the eye of the storm, before bursting forward with a speed that her feet seemed to conjure out of thin air.

Riley drove towards the makeshift basket, a hoop that had known her since she first dribbled a ball. As she approached, her focus was unwavering, her determination as clear as the evening sky above. With a final push, and spring into the air, she laid the ball up, watching as it kissed the backboard and fell gracefully through the net.

Breathing heavily, she retrieved the ball and stepped back to her starting position. This was more than practice; it was a promise to herself. Each repetition, each flawless execution of her favorite move, was a step closer to the player she aspired to be.

Back at the court, the Waves' meteoric rise had been a whirlwind of victories, their synergy growing stronger with each game. Riley and Jordan, the dynamic duo, were pivotal in these triumphs, their plays reflecting their deepening connection on the court.

In the midst of their success, Coach Ethan reminded them to stay grounded. "Victory is sweet, but it's the lessons we learn that build a team," he often said. The Waves, riding high on their winning streak, faced their next challenge with a blend of confidence and cautious anticipation – a game against the formidable Rebels.

The Greenwood Rebels, led by the Twins, Emily, and Olivia, were a force to be reckoned with. As the game commenced, the air in the gym was electric, charged with anticipation. The Waves quickly realized this game was different. Emily and Olivia's defense was relentless, their coordination uncanny. Riley's usually seamless dribbles were met with unrivaled pressure, while Jordan's sharp shots were deflected.

The Twins' prowess on the court tested every strategy the Waves had practiced. Jordan felt her usual confidence waver as each of her passes met stiff resistance. Riley, trying to navigate through the Rebels' defense, found her usual agility matched by the Twins' speed.

Coach Ethan's voice cut through their frustration during a timeout. "Remember, it's not just about scoring. It's about finding ways to adapt, to support each other." His words were calming, but the challenge remained daunting.

Despite their efforts, the Waves experienced their first-season loss. The defeat was a bitter pill to swallow, especially for Riley and Jordan, who were unaccustomed to such setbacks in their local clubs.

In the post-game huddle, Coach Ethan addressed the team, his tone serious yet encouraging. "Every game teaches us something. This loss is a lesson in resilience. We'll grow from it."

Riley and Jordan, both feeling the weight of responsibility, reflected on their performance. "I could've done better," Riley murmured, her disappointment evident. Jordan nodded in agreement, "We both could have. The Twins threw us off our game."

That week's practice was intense. Coach Ethan had them drill on new strategies, focusing on adaptability. The team rallied, their determination undiminished by the setback.

At the end of the practice, Coach Ethan's conversation with Riley and Jordan was both light-hearted and insightful.

"How do we feel the game went this week?" Coach questioned.

Disheartened, Riley answered, "I played a bad game".

Jordan's answer quickly followed, "Not good, I let the team down," she said looking towards the ground.

Expecting to be in trouble for how they played, the girls were both surprised at Ethan's response. "It was terrible! Nothing worked right?" laughed Ethan. The girls both started to laugh.

"What we need to remember is there are other ways to influence the game than just on the scoreboard," Ethan said reassuringly.

"When things aren't going your way, do the simple things, get your teammates involved, and be positive!" Riley and Jordan absorbed his words, a new resolve kindling within them. They laughed off the previous games' missteps, promising each other to learn and grow from the experience.

As Coach Ethan left, the girls lingered on the court, their spirits lifted. They were more than just teammates; they were partners in a journey filled with highs and lows, learning to navigate each twist and turn together.

CHAPTER 8:

BOUNCING BACK

The excitement of the local league games was palpable as Riley prepared to face her new Waves teammates, Maya and Alex, who played for the Hilltop Stars. Before leaving, Riley spent a quiet moment with her family. Her mum, sensing her nervous energy, questioned if everything was alright.

"I just get nervous when playing against my friends," Riley said sheepishly.

She gave her an encouraging smile. "Just do your best, Riley. We're proud of you, win or lose."

The drive to the game was a quiet one, but once at the stadium, Riley settled in with her team.
The first whistle blew, and the game tipped off with a burst of intensity. Riley, like a lightning bolt, zipped across the court, dribbling past Maya's lunging

defense to get to the basket and open the scoring. Then as quick as a flash, as Maya aimed a precision pass to Alex, Riley pounced with the agility of a cat, intercepting the ball mid-air. With a swift pivot, she was off, racing toward the basket and effortlessly sinking a layup. She felt a rush of exhilaration; the court was where she felt most alive.

As the game unfolded, Riley's brilliance continued to shine. A quick steal led to a seamless pass to a teammate, stationed at the three-point line, making the shot to put the game beyond doubt. Although the Stars fought hard, Riley's Wolves team, fuelled by her leadership and strategic plays, emerged victorious with a final score that echoed their dominance on the court.

Yet, amidst the cheers, she caught sight of Maya's disappointed frown and remembered what it was like to be on the losing side.

Across town, Jordan faced her own challenge, going head-to-head against Jess. Jordan's morning had started with a reflective walk with her dad, who had offered her advice: "Basketball is like life, Jordan. You'll face tough opponents, but it's how you play the game that counts."

Remembering her dad's words, Jordan played with determination, her strength and finesse on full display as she scored past Jess with a powerful drive. Jordan muscled through Jess's towering defense, unleashing a layup that seemed to defy gravity. The crowd gasped in awe at the sheer strength and determination on display. Jordan's basket ignited a spark in her team, setting the tone for an electrifying game. As the final buzzer sounded, Jordan's team celebrated a hard-fought win.

Days later, despite their local league showdowns the Waves enthusiastically reunited. As the game played out Alex's defensive prowess shone, her anticipation disrupting the opponents' rhythm. Riley watched in admiration, realizing there was much she could learn from Alex's strategic approach.

Maya's sharpshooting was another highlight. Positioned at the three-point line, she received a pass from Riley. With a flick of her wrist, the ball sailed through the air, arcing toward the basket. The swish of the net echoed through the gym as Maya's three-pointer added crucial points to the scoreboard. Watching the ball sail through the net, Riley felt a surge of pride for her teammate's skill and her role in enabling it.

As the game reached its climax, Riley and Jordan took center stage. A quick exchange of passes between them created an opening in the defense. Riley, demonstrating her ninja-like agility, darted through the opposition, leaving defenders in her wake. With a precise bounce pass, she found Jordan in the paint, who, with a quick step scored two points. The crowd erupted in cheers as the Waves clinched victory, their spirits soaring after overcoming challenges and showcasing the true power of teamwork.

After the game, Coach Ethan's pride was evident. "Great work, everyone. Riley, Jordan, you're growing into fine leaders. Maya, Alex, Jess – your contributions are invaluable. Remember, we're stronger together."

Post-game, on their travels home the team gathered in a local diner, a tradition after away games. Amidst burgers and fries, they shared stories from school, family life, and dreams beyond basketball. Riley, attending a different school than most of her teammates, listened intently to their school tales, laughing and sharing her own experiences.

Jordan, usually more reserved, opened up about a challenging project at school. "It's not all about basketball," she admitted. "Balancing everything is tough." Her teammates nodded in agreement, each sharing their strategies for juggling sports and academics.

As they left the diner, Riley and Jordan walked together, their conversation drifting from basketball to their aspirations, families, and the challenge of maintaining friendships. They realized their bond was rooted not just in their shared love for basketball but in their parallel journeys as young athletes.

The victory on the court was sweet, but it was these moments of connection and shared experiences that truly highlighted the essence of their journey. As Riley and Jordan parted ways, each heading to their respective homes, they knew that their paths, though different, were interwoven with the same thread of ambition, dedication, and the pursuit of dreams.

CHAPTER 9:

CHALLENGES AND TRIUMPHS

As the team stretched and cooled down in a quieter moment after practice, Riley, a little frustrated with herself after making some basic mistakes during the session, sat slumped against the wall as the rest of the team stretched. Her eyes followed her teammates, noticing their easy chatter and laughter. It was Jordan who first broke the silence, playfully teasing Jess about her flawlessly executed plays in practice.

The mood lightened, and soon, the girls were sharing stories and experiences from their basketball journeys. Amidst the laughter and shared memories, Riley nudged Jess gently, curious about her early days in basketball. This opened the door for Jess to share her own story, revealing a side of her journey that few knew – her struggle with anxiety in her early basketball days and how she overcame it to become the player she was today."Jess, what about you? How did you start in basketball?"

Jess took a deep breath, her eyes reflecting a mix of nostalgia and triumph. "Well, it wasn't easy for me," she began, her voice soft but clear. "When I first started playing basketball, I was incredibly anxious. I loved the game, but the moment I stepped on the court, I'd just freeze up. It was like my mind went blank, and my feet wouldn't move."

The girls leaned in, listening intently. Jess's usual confidence on the court seemed in stark contrast to the vulnerability she was revealing.

"I remember this one game," Jess continued, "I was so nervous, I couldn't even take a shot. I just passed the ball the moment it touched my hands. After the game, I felt so embarrassed. I almost gave up on basketball."

"But you didn't," Jordan interjected, admiration in her voice.

Jess smiled, a glimmer of pride in her eyes. "No, I didn't. I realized that my fear of making mistakes was holding me back. So, I started to work on my mindset. Every practice, I'd focus on just one thing – not the crowd, not the pressure, just the game."

Riley squeezed Jess's hand encouragingly. "And look at you now, one of the best players on our team."

Jess laughed, a genuine, contented sound. "It took a lot of practice, not just in playing but in believing in myself. I had to learn to embrace the nerves and channel them into my game. Now, when I step onto the court, I feel excited, not scared. Basketball has taught me so much more than just how to shoot a ball."

The girls sat in comfortable silence, each reflecting on Jess's story. It was a powerful reminder of their personal journeys and the challenges they had each overcome. This shared vulnerability deepened their bond, extending it beyond mere teamwork into genuine friendship and mutual respect.

As the team gathered their belongings and began to head out, Riley found herself contemplating not just Jess's story, but her own path in basketball. The court was where she felt most alive, her challenges transformed into opportunities. Yet, she couldn't help but think about the delicate balance she needed to maintain between her sport and her life outside the gym.

The rest of the week raced by with the regular routine of school, local league basketball, practice, and study and soon enough it was game day for the Waves.

After their recent win, the Waves entered a patch of great basketball form. In the first game of their winning streak, Riley's skills shone brightly. Her crossovers and agile movements bewildered defenders, paving the way for impressive plays. The thrill of the game, the roar of the crowd – it was here that Riley felt her worries melt away, her focus narrowing to the court and the game she loved.

Later, at home, a quick glance at her school books reminded Riley of the other important part of her life – her studies. While basketball was her passion, she knew that keeping up with her academics was crucial. It was a thought she tucked away in the back of her mind, a reminder of the responsibilities waiting for her once the final buzzer sounded.

Jordan, too, found challenges beyond the court. Her struggle to balance basketball with her social life was becoming more apparent.

As the winning streak continued, Riley showcased her scoring prowess, weaving through defenses like a maestro orchestrating a symphony. Jordan, a defensive powerhouse, dominated the boards and thwarted opponents with tenacity. Their connection on the court became the team's driving force, a beacon of inspiration for their teammates.

As the Waves prepared to face the Sunset Valley Titans, the air was thick with anticipation. The Titans' star player, Sienna, was a formidable opponent, her skills a mirror to Riley and Jordan's. The game was a battle of wits and agility, with Sienna's strategic plays challenging the Waves like never before.

As the clock ticked down, the intensity on the court escalated correspondingly. The Waves, in perfect sync, executed their plays with precision. Maya, always the impeccable shooter, found her spot beyond the arc and let fly a three-pointer that swished through the net, igniting cheers from the crowd. On defense, Alex's sharp instincts shone as she disrupted the Titans' rhythm, her hands quick and her feet quicker, stealing the ball and igniting a fast break.

The Titans, led by Sienna's relentless drive, answered back with their own barrage of skillful plays. Sienna, with her superb ball-handling, weaved through the Waves' defense, scoring a layup that drew gasps from the spectators. The game was a high-octane chess match, with each team countering the other's moves with tactical precision.

In this whirlwind of action, Jess, the quiet force for the Waves, made her presence felt. With a critical rebound off a missed free throw, she passed the ball to Riley, setting in motion the play that would widen the gap in the score. The teamwork was exemplary, a testament to their bond and collective resolve to rise to the challenge.

In the game's final minutes, the score was neck and neck. Riley's determination shone through as she intercepted a crucial pass, leading to a quick score. Her recent focus on academics paying off, her mind sharper and more focused than ever. Jordan, recognising the weight of the moment, pushed through fatigue. Her clutch plays finishing at the rim, as well as making free throws saw the Waves take a narrow, yet unreachable lead heading into the final seconds of the game.

Though Sienna matched their efforts, the Waves emerged victorious, their winning streak intact. The gym erupted in cheers, celebrating not just a win but the team's spirit and tenacity.
Post-game, Coach Ethan gathered the team. "You've shown true grit today. Remember, basketball is more than just the game; it's a reflection of life. The balance you maintain, the challenges you overcome, they all contribute to your growth as players and individuals."

The Waves, fuelled by their recent challenges and triumphs, looked ahead to the rest of the season with newfound determination. The journey was far from over, but with Riley and Jordan leading the way, the path was paved with the promise of more victories and the sweet taste of success.

CHAPTER 10:

OUCH!

At practice one afternoon, always wanting to keep his players thinking about the game, Coach Ethan called the team in for a huddle. "We've got a big game coming up, and we need to sharpen our defense," he announced, looking around at his team. "Alex, you've got some great ideas about our plays. Why don't you share them with the team?"

Alex nodded, a bit nervous but ready. She had spent hours studying their playbook and knew every move by heart. "Okay, team," she started, her voice steady. "Remember, defense is all about teamwork. We need to communicate and make sure we're all covering not just our players, but each others as well."

Riley watched Alex explain the strategies, impressed by how much she knew about the game. It wasn't just on the court that Alex worked hard. She was the same in school, always studying and getting good grades.

After the huddle, Riley bounced the ball over to Alex. "Hey, you did great there. How do you keep up with school and basketball like you do?" she asked.

Alex caught the ball and smiled. "Well, it's not easy. But I just try to stay organized and work hard. Basketball and school are both important to me, so I give my best to both."

Riley nodded, impressed. Alex wasn't just good at making plans for basketball; she was good at making plans for life, too.

Alex didn't realize it, but she was the heart of the Waves' lineup, a force to be reckoned with both on the court and in the classroom. Her friends often marveled at how her academic brilliance mirrored her basketball prowess. To them, Alex was the epitome of dedication and meticulous preparation.

From a young age, Alex had approached everything with a singular focus and determination. Her grades were a testament to her hard work and discipline. She spent countless hours poring over textbooks, her notes a colorful canvas of knowledge. But it wasn't just about getting good grades; for Alex, learning was a passion, an endless pursuit of excellence.

This same drive spilled over onto the basketball court. Alex was the strategist of the team, her mind always two steps ahead. She studied plays with the same intensity she devoted to her academics, understanding not only her role but every player's responsibility. Her teammates relied on her to dissect the opponent's strategy, to find weaknesses, and to adapt their gameplay mid-match.

On the court, Alex's leadership shone brightly. Her voice, clear and confident, could be heard over the squeak of sneakers and the thud of the basketball. She was the encourager, the motivator, always ready with a word of support or a tactical suggestion. When she was on the bench, her eyes never left the game, her mind working overtime, analyzing plays, and preparing feedback for her coach and teammates.

Defense was where Alex truly excelled. She relished the challenge of shutting down the opponent's best player, her movements a blend of grace and grit. Offensively, she was selfless, always looking to set up her teammates for the best shot. Her passes were precise, her vision of the court unparalleled.

Yet, for all her strengths, Alex was her own harshest critic. She held herself to incredibly high standards, both in basketball and in her studies. Her drive for perfection was a double-edged sword, pushing her to excel but also weighing heavily on her shoulders.

Despite the pressure she placed on herself, Alex thrived. She was the heartbeat of the Waves, the bridge between individual talent and team success.

Her mantra was simple: prepare, perform, perfect. It was a cycle she lived by, a rhythm that defined her path in sports and in life.

As she led the team chant after game breaks, her voice steady and strong, it was clear that Alex was more than just a player. She was a leader, a thinker, and a relentless pursuer of excellence. In Alex, the Waves had not just a player, but a guide, someone who embodied the spirit of the game and the pursuit of greatness.

As they returned to practice, Riley thought about what Alex said. She realized that being a part of a team meant learning from each other, not just about basketball, but about how to handle challenges off the court too.

Between the echoes of bouncing basketballs and the sharp whistle of the coach, the Waves' practice session wound down, each player carrying their intensity and focus off the court. As they gathered their gear, their minds were already transitioning from the hard work of practice to the anticipation of the upcoming game. They knew that each training session, each piece of advice from Alex, and each shared moment of determination was a step toward something greater.

With the game on the horizon, the atmosphere shifted from the controlled environment of practice to the unpredictable and exhilarating arena of competition. The Waves were ready, their unity solidified, their spirits high, prepared to face whatever challenges the game would bring.

As the players gathered pregame the gym was alive with the electric energy of anticipation as the Waves prepared for their game. Teammates exchanged encouraging smiles, and Jordan, a pivotal force on the team, took her position with confidence. The game started with the Waves' well-oiled teamwork, but an unexpected turn of events was about to unfold.

As Jordan received a pass near the basket, she collided with a defender. The gym hushed as Jordan fell, clutching her ankle in pain. Concerned whispers filled the space as Coach Ethan and the trainer rushed to her side. Riley watched, her heart sinking, as her friend and teammate was helped off the court.

The Waves were suddenly without one of their key players. In the stands, Jordan's parents exchanged worried glances, mirroring the team's concern. On the bench, Jordan sat, frustration etched on her face as she watched the game, her ankle throbbing.

Despite the setback, the Waves rallied. Riley, recognising the need to step up, took control of the game. Her agility and strategic thinking shone through as she navigated the heightened defense of the opposing team. Her much practiced behind the back dribble and drive move working like a charm to unlock the defense and create scoring opportunities. With every precise pass and calculated move, she filled the gap left by Jordan's absence.

Maya, seizing the moment, showcased her impeccable shooting skills, her three-pointers drawing cheers from the crowd. The team's unity was more apparent than ever, each member stepping up their game in response to the challenge they faced.

In the final moments, Riley's determination culminated in a drive through the defense, scoring a crucial basket helping to seal the win. The victory was a bittersweet triumph – a win overshadowed by the concern for Jordan.

As the team celebrated, Coach Ethan commended them. "You've shown incredible resilience today. This win speaks volumes about your character and unity as a team." He then turned to Riley, acknowledging her leadership, "You rose to the occasion, Riley. Well done."

On the sidelines, Jordan watched the celebrations, her emotions a complex mix of pride for her team and personal disappointment. Coach Ethan approached, his concern genuine. "How are you holding up, Jordan?"

Her response was a mix of frustration and resolve. "It's tough, Coach. I feel like I let the team down by not being out there."

Coach Ethan offered a reassuring smile. "Injuries are part of the sport. What matters is how you come back from them. Take this time to heal, and you'll be back stronger."

Jordan nodded, a determined glint in her eyes. "I'll be back, Coach. You can count on that."
As the teams cleared and court emptied Coach Ethan motioned for Alex to stay back for a moment. The gym was quieter now, the sounds of dribbling basketballs and squeaking sneakers fading as the players headed out.

"Alex, I wanted to talk to you," Coach Ethan began, his tone serious yet encouraging. "With Jordan out, the team's going to look to you even more. Your leadership has always been important, but now, it's crucial."

Alex nodded, understanding the weight of Coach Ethan's words. "I know, Coach. I'll do my best. Jordan's shoes are big to fill, but I won't let the team down."

Coach Ethan smiled, his confidence in Alex unwavering. "I know you won't. You have a natural ability to see the game and make smart decisions. The team respects you, not just for your skills, but for how you support them. Keep doing what you're doing, and we'll get through this together."

Alex felt a surge of determination and pride. She knew her role was about more than just playing well; it was about being a pillar her teammates could lean on, especially now.
"Thanks, Coach. I'm ready for the challenge," Alex replied, her voice steady.

As she walked away, her mind was already racing with strategies and encouragement for her teammates. This was her moment to step up, to be the leader her team needed.

CHAPTER 11:

MISSING PIECES

One sunny afternoon, Riley and Jordan decided to take a break from basketball and unwind with a leisurely walk through the local park. Jordan, her ankle still hurting from her recent injury, moved carefully, her steps measured but determined.

As they strolled, chatting about upcoming games and sharing laughs, they stumbled upon the soccer fields. There, to their surprise, they spotted Maya, engaged in a rigorous training session with her mother.

"Hey, isn't that Maya?" Riley pointed out, noticing her teammate's impressive footwork on the soccer field.

Jordan nodded, a hint of longing in her eyes as she watched Maya play. "Yeah, she's incredible. I can't wait to be back on the court... or any field, for that matter."

On the field, Maya moved with grace and agility, her connection with the ball almost poetic. Her mother, ever the supportive figure, passed the ball and offered pointers, her encouragement ringing clear across the field.

"Hey, Maya!" Riley called out, her voice carrying over the distance.

Maya, spotting her friends, jogged over, her eyes bright with enthusiasm. "Riley, Jordan! What a surprise! How are you doing?"

"We're good, just taking a stroll. But we couldn't help but stop and admire your skills," Riley said, grinning.

Jordan smiled, shifting her weight gently off her injured ankle. "You're amazing, Maya. Watching you play is a real treat."

Maya chuckled, wiping a bead of sweat from her forehead. "Thanks! I love soccer, but basketball has its own thrill, you know? Plus, I get to play with an awesome team."

As Maya talked about her love for both sports, Riley and Jordan saw a different side of her – the dedicated athlete who excelled in every sport she played, yet had to work doubly hard on her academics.

Maya's mum joined the group, her eyes immediately drawn to Jordan's ankle. "How's the ankle feeling, Jordan? It's going to be tough watching from the sidelines."

Jordan sighed, a mix of frustration and hope in her gaze. "Ahh not great, but slow and steady, right? The team's not going to be the same without me, though," she added with a playful smirk.

"You'll be back before you know it," Maya's mum assured her warmly. "And Maya here can learn a thing or two about patience and recovery from you."

Maya nodded in agreement. "Definitely. We all miss you on the team, Jordan. Your spirit's irreplaceable. But taking the time to heal properly now means you'll come back stronger."

As they chatted, the conversation flowed naturally from Maya's soccer training to Jordan's recovery and the upcoming basketball challenges. In that moment, the bond between the teammates was palpable—not just as athletes, but as friends supporting each other through every high and low.

As the Waves prepared for their upcoming games without Jordan, the gym was a mix of determination and uncertainty. Jordan, sidelined with her injury, watched from the stands, her presence a silent encouragement to her teammates.

The diagnosis of Jordan's injury was not good news as she would be missing for at least 3 games and with a tough schedule of games over that period the girls knew it was going to be a challenging road ahead.

Coach Ethan worked tirelessly to recalibrate the team. Maya and Alex, stepping out of Jordan's shadow, embraced new responsibilities, their versatility coming to the forefront. Jess, the towering center, found herself in a pivotal role, her defensive skills more crucial than ever.

Riley felt the pressure acutely. Each practice session, she pushed herself harder, her mind buoyed by Jordan's words of encouragement. "You got this, girl!" Jordan's text read, and Riley clung to that affirmation, determined to meet her friend's belief in her.

Off the court, the team rallied around Jordan. They organized study sessions at her house, ensuring she was engaged in her school projects and any team discussions they had. These moments, filled with laughter kept Jordan's spirits up and maintained her sense of belonging.

The day of the game arrived with a palpable tension. The Waves, now a rearranged puzzle, faced their opponents with a blend of apprehension and resolve. The gym, echoing with the buzz of anticipation, felt the void left by Jordan's absence.

As the game progressed, Maya and Alex shone in their new roles, their skills keeping the team afloat. Jess's dominance in the paint was a reminder of her growth, her confidence bolstering the team's defense.

Riley, channeling her inner strength and Jordan's inspiring messages, orchestrated the plays with a newfound maturity. Her eyes often met Jordan's on the bench, drawing silent support.

The game's final moments were a whirlwind. Down by one, Riley sprinted down the court. Maya and Alex trailed behind, searching for an opening. With time expiring in a split-second decision, Riley pulled up for a mid-range shot. The ball left her fingertips, sailing through the air as the buzzer sounded. As the ball bounced off the back of the rim, and away from the basket the reality of the missed shot was heart-wrenching.

The collective groan of disappointment resonated through the gym as the opposing team celebrated their narrow victory. Coach Ethan, though visibly disappointed, gathered the team, emphasizing the importance of resilience.

"You showed heart out there and we played hard. This isn't just about wins and losses; it's about how we face challenges and grow. We don't want to use not having Jordan as an excuse, Let's use this experience, to learn how we can improve and become stronger."

Riley, grappling with the mixed emotions of the loss and her role as a leader, found solace in her teammates' support. Maya and Alex, recognizing Riley's efforts, reassured her with encouraging words.

Meanwhile, Jordan, watching her team from the sidelines, felt a mix of pride and frustration. She longed to be on the court but knew the importance of recovery. Her resolve to return stronger was fueled by her team's perseverance.

The Waves left the gym that day with a renewed sense of purpose. The setback was hard, but it was a part of their journey – a journey of growth, resilience, and unbreakable team spirit.

CHAPTER 12:

A WARRIOR'S RESOLVE

At the crack of dawn, Riley awoke to the soft chirping of birds and the gentle rustle of leaves outside her room. The air at the school camp was crisp and invigorating, filling her lungs with a sense of adventure as she stepped out to greet the day. Although a little tired from a night filled with whispers and quiet giggles hidden away from teacher's ears, she was ready for the day's activities. The camp, nestled in a lush forest, was a world away from the polished hardwood floors of the basketball court, offering a different kind of challenge and excitement.

Each day unfolded with a new adventure. Riley found herself scaling rock walls, her fingers gripping the rough edges as she learned to trust her strength and instincts. The afternoons were spent canoeing on the serene lake, the rhythmic splash of paddles syncing with her heartbeat, reminding her of the importance of teamwork and coordination.

The highlight of the camp was the night hike, a journey under the starlit sky that felt like navigating through a different realm. Armed with only flashlights and the guidance of their instructors, Riley and her classmates tread softly through the whispering woods. Every crunch of twigs underfoot, every rustle in the bushes, added to the thrill, igniting a sense of wonder and camaraderie among them.

As they reached a clearing, the group gathered around a crackling campfire, the flames casting a warm glow on their faces. They shared stories and roasted marshmallows, the laughter and shared moments forging bonds that transcended the usual school interactions. Riley realized that these connections, these shared triumphs, and challenges, were not so different from what she experienced with her basketball team.

Camp was more than an escape from the ordinary; it was a journey of growth, discovery, and friendship. As Riley lay in her sleeping bag each night, the canopy of stars above her, she felt a profound gratitude for these experiences, knowing they were shaping her not just as a player, but as a person ready to face any challenge, on or off the court.

Returning from her school camp, Riley carried with her a mosaic of memories – the laughter around the campfire, the challenging hikes, and the camaraderie of her classmates. These experiences were still fresh in her mind as she stepped off the bus, the scent of damp earth lingering in her senses. But there was little time to rest; a basketball game awaited her.

At home, Riley shared stories of her adventures with her family. Her parents listened intently, smiling at her tales, but they could see the fatigue in her eyes. "Make sure you're up for the game, Riley," her mum cautioned gently.

En route to the game, the rhythmic hum of the car lulled Riley into a brief nap, her dreams a blend of camp adventures and basketball courts. Waking up to the familiar sights and sounds of the gym, she shook off the remnants of sleep, steeling herself for the game ahead.

On the court, the fatigue from her time at camp weighed heavily on Riley. Each dribble in the warm-up felt slower, each jump harder. Yet, as the game commenced, an inner switch flipped within her. The presence of her parents in the stands, the encouraging glances from Coach Ethan, and the absence of Jordan's supportive figure on the court fuelled her resolve.

The Waves faced the Comets, a team known for their skill and agility. Gemma, the Comets' star player, was a formidable opponent, but Riley was undeterred. She channeled her camp-inspired resilience, darting past defenders with a burst of energy that belied her exhaustion.

Throughout the game, Riley's performance was nothing short of remarkable. She seemed to be everywhere – stealing balls, scoring baskets, and rallying her team. Maya and Alex adapted their gameplay to support Riley, while Jess's dominance in defense was a rock for the team.

Coach Ethan, watching Riley's relentless drive, offered tactical advice and constant encouragement. "Keep pushing, Riley! You can do this," he shouted, his voice full of admiration for her grit. Riley, knowing her team needed her went to a whole new level of ability.

As the game intensified, Riley's presence on the court became undeniable. With each possession, she seemed to elevate her game to new heights. With the ball in her hands, she orchestrated the offense with poise and precision. On one play, she executed a flawless behind-the-back dribble to shake her defender, driving toward the basket with unstoppable momentum. Her layup was a masterpiece of agility and finesse, the ball spinning off the glass and into the net with a satisfying swish.

Not content with just offensive prowess, Riley showcased her defensive skills too. She moved like a shadow, anticipating her opponent's every move. With quick feet and keen eyes, she stole the ball mid-pass, igniting a fast break. Down the court she flew, ball in hand, eyes fixed on the hoop. She feinted left, then crossed over to her right, leaving her defender a step behind. With a powerful leap, she rose above the outstretched hands of the opposing team and released the ball at the apex of her jump. The crowd erupted as the ball sailed through the hoop, her athleticism and skill on full display.

These moments of individual brilliance were punctuated by her teamwork. She connected with Alex on intricate plays, her passes crisp and perfectly timed. With Jess setting solid screens and Maya cutting to the basket with precision, Riley found them with pinpoint accuracy, leading to easy scores. As the game clock ticked down, Riley's contributions had turned the tide, her talent and leadership propelling the team forward with every play.

As the final moments ticked down, Riley's last shot – a bid to clinch victory – was a testament to her sheer willpower. Coming off a screen set by Maya, Riley turned and attacked the basket, piercing through the defense in trademark fashion. The ball kissed off the backboard and fell through the rim, her effort was met with roaring applause from the crowd and her teammates.

Post-game, as the team walked out of the stadium, Coach Ethan walked next to Riley, placing a reassuring hand on her shoulder, he, said "That was one of my favorite games ever. You're something special, kid"

Exhausted, Riley smiled, full of pride.

Once back in the car, Riley's parents were raving to her about the game!

"Oh my goodness, that was incredible Riley!" her Dad exclaimed.
Riley, her energy finally spent, could only offer a tired smile in response. As her mum turned to share her excitement, she found Riley already fast asleep, a peaceful contrast to the warrior she had been on the court.

In that moment of quiet, Riley's parents exchanged a look of pride and admiration. Their daughter, growing with every challenge, was not just a basketball player; she was proving to be a young woman of remarkable strength and character.

CHAPTER 13:

ECHOES OF DEFEAT

The week preceding the rematch with the Greenwood Rebels was a whirlwind of rigorous training and local league games. Riley, fresh off her remarkable performance, juggled her school responsibilities with basketball, her energy a testament to her dedication. Yet, the looming challenge of facing the Rebels without Jordan weighed heavily on her mind.

Coach Ethan, recognizing the gap left by Jordan's absence, fine-tuned strategies to leverage the team's strengths. In his candid talks with Jordan, he emphasized the importance of her health over haste. "Your recovery is crucial. We need you at your best, not just back," he advised.

Jordan, observing from the sidelines, felt a complex mix of pride and helplessness. Watching Maya, Alex, and Jess adapt to new roles, she ached to rejoin them, yet understood the necessity of her recovery. Each game she missed fueled her resolve to return stronger.

As the rematch day dawned, the gymnasium was charged with a mix of anticipation and apprehension. The absence of Jordan's dynamic presence was palpable, a silent echo in every dribble and pass.

The game began with the Waves struggling to find their rhythm. Maya, thrust into a more prominent role, grappled with the pressure, her usual precision slightly off-mark. Alex, facing the relentless offense of the Rebels, navigated through the game with determination but missed the synchronicity she shared with Jordan. Jess, despite her best efforts in the paint, found herself outmaneuvered by the Twins.

Coach Ethan's instructions from the sidelines struggled to penetrate the mounting frustration. The Twins, with their seamless coordination, exploited every gap, their synergy a stark contrast to the Waves' disjointed efforts.

Sitting among the spectators, Jordan clenched her fists, feeling every missed shot and lost rebound as her own. She saw the strain in Riley's eyes, the burden of leadership in Jordan's absence a weight upon her shoulders.

As the final buzzer sealed the Waves' defeat, a solemn mood enveloped the team. The loss was more than a score; it was a reflection of their current struggles and the void left by Jordan.

In the locker room, Coach Ethan addressed the somber faces. "This defeat is tough, but it's a part of our journey. Let's use this as a learning opportunity. We'll come back stronger, more unified." His gaze lingered on Riley, whose efforts to rally the team hadn't gone unnoticed.

Riley, feeling the sting of defeat, knew it was her responsibility to uplift the team. "We'll get through this together," she said, her voice firm yet supportive. The team nodded, their resolve reigniting despite the setback.

Jordan approached Coach Ethan, her determination clear. "I'm going to be back for the next game, Coach. I can't watch this from the sidelines anymore."

Coach Ethan, seeing the fire in Jordan's eyes, knew her return could be the catalyst the team needed. "We'll assess your recovery, Jordan. If you're ready, your return could be the turning point we need."

As the team dispersed, the echoes of defeat lingered, but so did a growing sense of anticipation. Jordan's potential return and Riley's unwavering leadership hinted at a new chapter for the Waves, one where challenges were met with unyielding spirit and teamwork.

CHAPTER 14:

HESITANT HOMECOMING

As Jordan sat on the sidelines, her ankle securely wrapped in a bandage, a mix of frustration and determination in her eyes. The hustle of each game echoed around her, a stark reminder of where she longed to be – back on the court with her team. The injury had been a harsh setback, but Jordan was not one to dwell on misfortune. Instead, she focused on her recovery, fueled by the unwavering resolve to rejoin her teammates as soon as possible.

Her visits to the physiotherapist became a regular part of her routine. Each session was challenging, pushing her to the limits of her endurance. The physio, a kind yet firm figure, guided her through a series of exercises designed to strengthen her ankle. Jordan embraced the pain and effort, knowing that each stretch, each strengthening exercise, brought her one step closer to her goal.

She clung to the physio's encouraging words, "Progress is a slow process, but your dedication will pay off."

At home, Jordan followed her recovery plan with meticulous attention. Ice packs, elevation, and gentle movements became part of her daily life. She visualized herself playing again, moving across the court with her usual agility and speed. This mental exercise kept her spirits high and her focus sharp. Her family supported her tirelessly, offering encouragement and celebrating every small sign of progress.

As days turned into weeks, Jordan's ankle gradually regained strength. She started to feel more like herself – a player ready to face the challenges of the game. Her determination never waned, and with each passing day, her motivation only grew stronger. Jordan knew the road back to the court would not be easy, but she was ready to embrace the journey with all the grit and resilience she possessed. "I'll be back stronger," she promised herself, her eyes reflecting the fire of an athlete unwilling to be held back by adversity.

After weeks of rigorous rehabilitation and unwavering determination, the day finally arrived when Jordan laced up her sneakers once more, her heart pounding with anticipation as she stepped onto the court, ready to make her comeback in the game she loved.

The gymnasium buzzed with a mix of excitement and trepidation as the Waves prepared for Jordan's return. Her teammates, while thrilled to have her back, couldn't help but notice the subtle changes in her movements – a hint of hesitation, a shade less of her usual confidence.

During warm-ups, Jordan's cautious steps spoke volumes. Riley caught Maya's eye, both sharing a silent understanding of the courage it took for Jordan to step back onto the court. Jess gave an encouraging nod, while Alex patted Jordan's back, a gesture of solidarity.

As the game started, the Waves faced the challenge of integrating Jordan back into their rhythm. The team worked to find a balance, adapting to Jordan's tentative play. Coach Ethan, keenly observing, made strategic adjustments, ensuring Jordan was supported but not overburdened.

Jordan's contributions, though more subdued than usual, were crucial. Her rebounds and assists, interspersed with flashes of her characteristic power, invigorated the team. Riley, in sync with Jordan, provided steady support, her plays mindful of Jordan's pacing.

A key moment unfolded when Riley, after a swift drive, passed the ball to Jordan. With a deep breath, Jordan took the shot and scored a small but significant victory. The bench erupted in cheers, not just for the basket, but for the symbolic triumph it represented.

Riley, seizing a quiet moment during a break, leaned in. "We've got this, Jordan. No pressure, just play your game," she whispered. Jordan's grateful smile was all the reply Riley needed.

The game progressed with the Waves demonstrating a resilience born of unity. Each player, in their own way, contributed to the fluidity of the game, compensating for the shifts in dynamics with Jordan's return.

The final buzzer sounded, marking a hard-earned victory. The cheers that filled the gym were as much for the win as for the milestone Jordan had crossed. The team huddled, their spirits high, with Coach Ethan offering words of encouragement. "Today was about more than basketball. It was about courage, about coming together as a team. Jordan, your bravery in stepping back onto this court makes us all stronger."

After the game, as the gym emptied, Riley joined Jordan, her expression one of admiration. "You were amazing out there. It's great to have you back," she said. Jordan, her emotions a mix of relief and joy, responded, "Thanks, Riley. It feels good, but I've still got a way to go."

Coach Ethan joined them, his pride evident. "You took an important step today, Jordan. Hopefully, you'll pull up okay from tonight's game so you can get back to your normal self. We've got your back though, until you're 100%."He offered her a supportive fist bump, a small gesture that spoke volumes of his trust and confidence in her journey back.

As they left the gym, the Waves knew that their journey would have more challenges, but with Jordan's return and the bond they shared, they were ready to face whatever came next – together.

CHAPTER 15:

THE PARTY AND THE PIVOT

Riley's locker echoed through the busy hallway as she secured it shut, turning to find Emma, her school friend, approaching with an excitement that was almost tangible. "Riley, you've got to come to my party on the weekend! Everyone's talking about it," Emma exclaimed, extending a glittering invitation.

The idea of a party, a night of laughter and music, was tempting to Riley. A rare escape from the rigor and routine of basketball. "That sounds awesome, Em," she said, her face lighting up at the thought.

Throughout the day, the party buzzed in Riley's mind like a catchy tune. She pictured herself there, free from the weight of her athletic responsibilities, just a regular girl enjoying a fun night at a party.

But later, at home, reality cast a long shadow over her daydreams. Riley sat on her bed, basketball in hand, the invitation lying forgotten beside her. The Waves had a game scheduled for the same time as Emma's party – not just any game, but one that could define their season. The thought of not being there, not fighting alongside her team, gnawed at her.

Riley's parents noticed her pensive mood at dinner. Her dad broke the silence, "You seem a million miles away, Riley. Something on your mind?"

Riley hesitated, then shared her dilemma. Her mum listened thoughtfully before speaking, "Riley, we're proud of how dedicated you are to basketball, but it's okay to enjoy life outside of sports too."

Her dad nodded in agreement, "Life's about balance. We support you, whether you're on the court or at Emma's party. What matters is that you're happy with your choice."

Their words echoed in Riley's mind as she lay in bed that night, the decision weighing heavily on her. Basketball was more than a game to her; it was a passion, a commitment to herself and her team. Missing the game wasn't just about letting down her team; it was about letting down a part of herself.

The next morning, Riley approached Emma, her decision made. "I can't go to your party, Em. I've got a really important game," she said, trying to mask her disappointment.

Emma's face fell, a mix of confusion and disappointment. "But it's just one game, Riley. Can't you miss it for once?"

Riley shook her head, feeling the divide between her world and Emma's. "Basketball is a big part of who I am, Em. I can't just set it aside, not even for one night."

Emma nodded slowly, not fully grasping the depth of Riley's commitment, but respecting her decision nonetheless.

That weekend, as the Waves geared up for the game, Riley's mind briefly wandered to the party she was missing. But as soon as she stepped onto the court, her doubts faded away. The sound of the ball, the roar of the crowd, the adrenaline rush of the game – this was where she belonged.

Riley played one of her best games that night. Her focus was unwavering, each shot and pass a testament to her dedication to the sport and her team. When the final buzzer sounded, signaling a hard-fought victory for the Waves, Riley knew she had made the right choice.

Coach Ethan, recognizing her outstanding performance, pulled her aside. "Your dedication makes all the difference, Riley. Great job tonight."

The words filled Riley with pride and reassurance. She realized then that while sacrifices were part of being an athlete, they were worth it for moments like these.

After the game, as the gym slowly emptied and the sound of bouncing basketballs faded, Coach Ethan approached Riley. He wore a knowing expression, one that spoke of shared understanding and deeper insights.

"Riley, your parents told me about the party you missed for tonight's game," Ethan began, his voice carrying a blend of empathy and respect. "I know it wasn't easy, choosing between a fun night out and the game. But that decision, says a lot about you and your dedication."

Riley listened, her basketball still in hand, feeling the weight of her choice.

Ethan continued, "In life, and especially in sports, sacrifices are inevitable. What you gave up tonight, it's part of a much larger journey, one that could take you far in basketball. These choices, shape not just the athlete you become, but the person you are."

Riley nodded, her decision settling more comfortably within her. Ethan's words echoed the sentiments she felt but hadn't fully articulated.

"You're on a path that few have the discipline or courage to follow," Ethan added, his eyes reflecting the lights of the now quiet gym. "Someday, you might look back and see how these moments of sacrifice were stepping stones to something greater, maybe even something extraordinary in your basketball career."

Riley felt a surge of determination, mixed with a newfound understanding of the journey she was on. Ethan's acknowledgment of her sacrifice and his belief in her potential filled her with a sense of purpose.

"Thanks, Coach. It means a lot, hearing that from you," Riley said, her voice steady and more confident. "I'm ready for whatever comes next, on and off the court."

Leaving the court, Riley felt a sense of peace with her decision. She had the support of her family, the respect of her coach, and the camaraderie of her team.

On the drive home, the night alive with possibilities, Riley smiled to herself. There would be other parties and other dances, but the joy she found on the court was incomparable. She felt a renewed sense of commitment to her sport.

The path of an athlete was filled with tough choices, but it was hers, and she was ready to embrace it fully, driven by the promise of the journey ahead

CHAPTER 16:

RUN TO FINALS

The whistle blew, signaling the end of another intense practice session. As the gym's echoes faded, Riley and Jordan lingered, their basketballs tucked under their arms.

"Hey, no school tomorrow, right?" Riley asked, a mischievous glint in her eye.

"Yeah, student-free day!" Jordan confirmed, her excitement matching Riley's. "Sleepover at my place?"

"Let's do it! And let's invite Alex too. I heard her school's off as well."

The plan was set in motion with a flurry of messages and phone calls. Jordan's mom, ever the gracious host, agreed with a laugh, "Sure, but hosting three energetic basketball stars is no small feat!"

Riley's and Alex's parents echoed the sentiment, their voices laced with humor and a hint of admiration for the upcoming adventure.

The sleepover was an epic blend of laughter and chaos. They transformed the living room into a cozy fort, with blankets and pillows scattered everywhere. The night brimmed with movie marathons, a daring dance-off, and an ambitious attempt at baking cookies, which, despite their questionable shapes, tasted like victory.

Early in the morning hours, the sleepover turned into a strategy session. As they huddled under their blanket fort, the weight of the upcoming finals loomed large. "We've got to be at our best. Every play counts," Riley mused, the flicker of determination in her eyes visible even in the dim light.

Jordan, sharing an oddly shaped cookie, added, "We've come this far together. Let's make sure we finish strong."

As the three girls drifted off to sleep, Coach Ethan's words during the afternoon's practice session echoed in their minds. "These games are about more than just basketball. They're a testament to your resilience and your unity. Play our way, and the rest will follow."
The next day unfurled with the ease of a lazy summer breeze. They hit the local arcade, fiercely competing in air hockey and laughing through a round of ten-pin

bowling, as Riley sent down gutter ball after gutter ball.

"You may be good at basketball Riley, but bowling certainly is not your thing," Alex said with a laugh.

Lunch was a picnic in the park, a simple feast of hot chips under the canopy of the sunny sky. It was a day of unwinding, an important reminder of the joy found in moments shared with friends. This was especially important given the upcoming games.

The next few days flowed with the ease of relaxed minds and bodies as the Waves readied themselves for the challenge ahead.

The first game of the run toward the finals was a showcase of the Waves' tactical prowess. Jordan showing her trademark toughness to go with Riley's agility and sharp thinking set the tone, her lightning-fast steals turning defense into offense. Maya, with her pinpoint accuracy, and Alex, with her unwavering defense, complemented the dynamic duo perfectly.

In the second game, Jordan's resurgence was undeniable. Every rebound and drive was a statement of her return to form. Jess's control under the basket provided the perfect balance to Riley and Jordan's offensive onslaught.

The team huddled during a critical time-out in the penultimate game. Riley's voice cut through the tension, "We've got the momentum. Let's keep pushing!" Coach Ethan added, "Believe in your strength, and trust in each other."

The final game before the finals was a symphony of skill and teamwork. Alex's defensive mastery, Maya's three-pointers, and Jess's rebounds created a seamless flow, each player shining in their role, a testament to their hard work and dedication.

As the final buzzer sounded, signaling another victory, the gym erupted in celebration. The team's journey to the finals had been a rollercoaster of emotions, each player contributing to their collective success.

In the huddle after the game, Coach Ethan's eyes twinkled with pride. "You've shown what true teamwork is all about. The upcoming finals are not just a game; they're a chance to leave your mark. Let's go out there and show them what the Waves are made of."

The team united in their goal, left the gym with a renewed sense of purpose. For Riley and Jordan, the finals were more than a competition; they were the culmination of a journey filled with growth, challenges, and unbreakable bonds.

As they walked out into the night, the echoes of their laughter mingled with the anticipation of the challenge that lay ahead.

CHAPTER 17:

THE SHOWDOWN

In the lead-up to the Local League game of the season, Riley's and Jordan's parents exchanged friendly banter, a reflection of the lighthearted rivalry between their daughters.

"Bet you a coffee that Riley scores the first basket," Riley's mom teased Jordan's dad, her tone playful yet confident.

Jordan's dad chuckled, adjusting his cap. "You're on, but when Jordan makes a three-pointer, I expect a muffin with that coffee!"

Meanwhile, the group chat between the Waves teammates was buzzing with mock predictions and playful trash talk.

Alex's message popped up first: "Prediction: Jordan trips over her own shoelaces trying to guard Riley."
Maya quickly joined in: "Oh please, Riley's going to be so dizzy from Jordan's crossovers, she'll need a GPS to find the hoop!"

Jess sent a GIF of a referee, jokingly adding, "I'll be watching you two! No funny business or I'm calling fouls from the stands!."

Riley responded with a string of laughing emojis, her message following: "Just wait, I've got a move so secret, not even the FBI knows about it!"

Jordan chimed in with her usual competitive flair: "Bring it, Riley! We'll let our game do the talking! Just hope you're ready for my 'Jordan special'."

The chat was filled with playful jabs and laughter emojis, the perfect prelude to the friendly yet fierce rivalry about to unfold on the court. It was clear that no matter the outcome, the bond between the Waves was unbreakable, their friendship a testament to the true spirit of the game.

As the referee's whistle pierced the charged air, Riley and Jordan sprang into action. Riley, nimble and precise, wove through defenders with the agility that had become her trademark. Across the court, Jordan countered with her characteristic power, her rebounds, and drives a display of her unwavering determination.

Jess, Maya, and Alex watching from the sidelines, were torn between cheering for their teammates and marveling at the spectacle. Each play was a testament to Riley and Jordan's evolution from rivals to teammates and back again for this high-stakes game.

As the match progressed, so did the intensity. Riley's unparalleled athleticism clashed with

Jordan's sheer force. A fast break led to a heart-stopping moment at the basket, their competitive spirits on full display. The gym reverberated with the energy of their one-on-one duel, a dance of two athletes at the peak of their game.

With the score neck-and-neck, the final minutes became a battlefield of wits and skill. In a pivotal moment, Riley's deft footwork outmaneuvered Jordan, her spin move culminating in a decisive layup. The crowd erupted as the Wolves clinched a narrow victory.

Post-game, amidst the buzz of exhilarated spectators, Riley and Jordan met at mid-court. "Haha, got ya!" Riley exclaimed, her competitive smirk softened by the warmth of their friendship.

"Nice move, Riley," Jordan conceded with a playful nudge. "But next time, I've got your number."

Maya and Alex joined them, their laughter mingling with the gym's residual excitement. "You two better not have any more tricks up your sleeves. We need you both in top form for the Waves," Maya joked.

"Yeah, we've got big games coming up, and we need our dynamic duo united, not battling each other!" Alex chimed in, her tone light but filled with anticipation for their upcoming challenges.

Riley and Jordan exchanged a look of mutual respect and nodded. "Bring it on!" they responded in unison, their voices echoing a shared resolve.

The showdown, though a fierce competition, reinforced their bond. As they left the gym, the night air was alive with the promise of their continued journey, a journey marked by rivalry, friendship, and the unbreakable spirit of two athletes who had grown together, each pushing the other to greater heights.

CHAPTER 18:

POPCORN

On a rare weekend free from basketball, Riley, Maya, and Jess decided to catch the latest blockbuster at the local cinema. As they settled into their seats, munching on popcorn, Riley's gaze wandered and landed on a familiar duo a few rows ahead. "Isn't that Jordan and Alex?" she whispered, pointing discreetly.

Maya squinted and then grinned. "It is! Let's have a little fun." The trio giggled, formulating a mischievous plan. Quietly, they began tossing popcorn kernels, aiming for Jordan and Alex. Each successful hit was followed by suppressed laughter and ducking behind their seats.

At first, Jordan and Alex seemed oblivious, engrossed in the movie previews. But as more popcorn rained down, they caught on. Jordan turned around, her eyes scanning the darkened room, a smirk forming on her lips. Without a word, she and Alex grabbed their own popcorn boxes.

In a swift move, Jordan and Alex stood up, spun around, and launched a popcorn barrage towards the giggling trio behind them. The air filled with flying popcorn as both groups burst into laughter. The surrounding moviegoers began to complain, some chuckling at the absurdity of the popcorn fight.

Before they knew it, an usher, trying hard to maintain a stern face, approached them. "I'm sorry, but I have to ask you all to leave," he said, gesturing towards the exit. The girls, still laughing, gathered their belongings and exited the cinema, their plans to watch the movie forgotten in the wake of their popcorn escapade.

Outside the cinema, under the glow of the bright lights, the five girls shared a moment of uncontrollable laughter. "Well, that was worth it," Jordan exclaimed, wiping tears of mirth from her eyes. "Who needs a movie when you have friends like these?"

The laughter from the movie theater popcorn fiasco still lingered as Riley, Maya, Jess, Jordan, and Alex entered the gym for their next game. The atmosphere was filled with the usual pre-game tension, but for them, it was laced with the recent memory of their shared mischief.

As they began their warm-up drills, passing the ball back and forth, Maya pretended to dodge an imaginary piece of popcorn, dramatically throwing herself to the ground. "Watch out, incoming!" she exclaimed with a grin.

The reference instantly sparked laughter among the group. Jess, trying to maintain her dribbling, laughed so hard she nearly lost control of the ball. "I can't believe we got kicked out before the movie even started," she said, still chuckling.

Riley passed the ball to Jordan, who caught it while pretending to shield her head from popcorn. "Guess we're better at basketball than behaving in a cinema," Jordan joked, her eyes twinkling with amusement.

Alex, joining in the fun, added, "Next time, let's stick to a movie night at someone's house. Safer for everyone involved, especially the popcorn!"

Their laughter and light-hearted banter continued throughout the warm-up, easing the usual pre-game nerves. The incident not only provided them with a good laugh but also brought them closer as a team.

As the coach called them in for a final huddle before the game, the girls' faces were still lit up with smiles.

The popcorn episode had become their inside joke, a symbol of their unity and friendship both on and off the court.

Once in the huddle, the laughter and giggles quickly turned to sharp focus as the Bayside Waves prepared for their crucial showdown against the Sunset Valley Titans, the air was thick with anticipation. Coach Ethan, with his characteristic blend of focus and passion, laid out a meticulous plan to neutralize the Titans' star player, Sienna. Riley, Jordan, and the rest of the team listened intently, absorbing every detail of the strategy.

The plan to neutralize Sienna's impact was as follows:
1. Contain in the open court:
The Waves, led by Alex's defensive acumen, were to keep Sienna in front of them, and not let her get past them easily in the open court, limiting her ability to get to the basket for quick scores. Alex's swift movements and keen game sense were pivotal in executing this part of the plan.

2. Trap and Rotate:
If Sienna was to catch the ball from a pass, or come off a screen then the Waves would trap her by creating a double team. Riley's speed and Jordan's court awareness would come to the fore as they implemented the trapping strategy. Their coordinated effort, along with the rest of the team, would create a defensive net that would stifle Sienna's options.

3. Deny the Return Pass:

If Sienna didn't have the ball, the Waves, particularly Maya with her agility, would shadow her, denying her the chance to become a playmaker and not getting the ball back once she had passed the ball.

They broke the huddle, their spirits high and ready to face the challenge ahead. The popcorn incident had been a silly, spontaneous moment, but it had reinforced the strength of their bond – a bond that was about to be tested on the court.

Throughout the game, Coach Ethan's instructions from the sidelines were decisive and clear, guiding the Waves through each play. His ability to read the game and make on-the-spot decisions was a key factor in the team's performance.

The game itself was a thrilling display of skill and strategy. Riley's leadership on the court shone as she matched Sienna's agility and skill, while Jordan's presence in the paint was a constant threat to the Titans. Maya's and Alex's contributions were crucial, with Maya's sharp shooting and Alex's tenacious defense creating a solid foundation for the team's success.

Riley, with a swift crossover dribble, left her defender stumbling, creating an open lane for a quick layup.

The crowd erupted as the ball kissed the backboard and dropped through the net.

Maya, showcasing her defensive prowess, anticipated an opponent's pass, making a lightning-quick steal. With a burst of speed, she raced down the court, leaving Titans in her wake, and finished with a graceful finger roll.

Coach Ethan's voice cut through the intensity, guiding his players through the ebb and flow of the game. "Maya, deny on the press! Jordan, crash the boards! Riley, drive the lane!" The Waves executed their plays with precision. Maya intercepted a pass, triggering a fast break that culminated in Jordan's confident shot, eliciting cheers from the crowd.

Jordan, positioned in the post, received a precision pass from Riley. With a decisive pivot, she created separation from her defender and unleashed a hook shot that found nothing but net. The synchronized movement of the Waves left the Titans defense in disarray.

In a Titans fast break, Riley intercepted an errant pass, igniting a counterattack. She dribbled effortlessly, drawing defenders toward her. With a no-look pass, she found Maya on the wing, who sank a smooth jump shot, punctuating the sequence with finesse.

As the Titans attempted to press, Riley orchestrated a pick-and-roll with Jess. With a perfectly timed screen, Jess created space, and Riley, with a deceptive hesitation, exploited the opening for a mid-range jumper that swished through the basket. The Waves playbook unfolded like a well-choreographed dance, each play a testament to their chemistry and skill.

The Titans fought back fiercely, but the Waves responded with resilience. Jess, a force in the paint, boxed out opponents with authority. A rebound secured, she unleashed a thunderous outlet pass to Riley, setting the stage for another swift transition play.

Sienna, the Titans' star player, attempted to rally her team, but Alex's defensive prowess shone. Like a shadow, she mirrored Sienna's every move, disrupting passing lanes and forcing turnovers. A steal transitioned into a fast break, and Riley, with a burst of speed, finished with a dazzling layup that brought the crowd to its feet.

In the closing moments, with the score hanging in the balance, Jordan seized control. A series of dominant moves on the wing left the defence scrambling, as she powered through for crucial baskets.

As the final buzzer sounded, the Waves emerged victorious, their faces a picture of elation and relief. Coach Ethan's game plan had been executed to perfection, and the team's cohesion and adaptability were on full display.

In the post-game huddle, Coach Ethan's eyes gleamed with pride. "That was a masterclass in teamwork and strategic play," he praised. "You all stepped up, played your parts brilliantly, and showed what the Waves are capable of. This victory is yours, and it's well-deserved."

However, the celebration was tempered with the knowledge that the journey was far from over. Coach Ethan quickly refocused the team on the upcoming challenges. "We presume we've got the Comets next in the Semi Final, and they won't be easy. But if we play like we did today, with the same determination and teamwork, we'll make it to the final."

The team's response was a unified chorus of determination. They were ready for the next challenge, their eyes set on the ultimate prize - the championship.

"Let's keep this momentum going," Coach Ethan concluded, his voice filled with conviction as he glanced at Alex.

"Waves on three" Alex began enthusiastically. "One, two, three, Waves!" The team yelled with pride.

As they broke the huddle, Coach Ethan quipped with a laugh, "Now, who wants Popcorn?" Riley, Jordan,

Maya, Alex, and the rest of the team broke out in hysterics again as they walked off the court, united in their quest for glory, each step bringing them closer to their dream of winning the finals.

CHAPTER 19:

THE UNEXPECTED CLASH

In the days leading up to the next game, the Waves adopted a cautious approach outside of basketball. Conversations between school friends in the hallways revolved around preserving energy and avoiding unnecessary risks. Riley and Jordan, the dynamic duo, exchanged messages during the week sharing both the nerves, excitement, and determination at facing off against Gemma in the Semi Final.

As the players walked into the gym for their training session ahead of their big clash, they found Coach Ethan waiting for them mid court.

"Team, we've got news." his voice cutting through the air, signaling a shift in focus. The Comets threw a curveball and beat the Rebels! So, instead of the Comets, who we thought we'd be playing, we'll be facing the Rebels in the Semi-Finals instead."

A hush fell over the team as they absorbed the unexpected twist. The Rebels had comprehensively beaten the Waves the last time they met, and the twins posed an exceptional challenge. Disappointment lingered briefly, but Coach Ethan's steady gaze and reassuring words rekindled their determination. "This changes nothing. We've faced the Rebels before, and we know what it takes to beat them. Adjust your mindset, stay focused, and let's rewrite our story against them."

The news rippled through the team, and a newfound resolve set in.

Coach Ethan, recognizing the shift in dynamics, rallied the team with a strategic training session. "We adapt and overcome. Our goal remains the same, and it starts with training. We know the Rebels, and we'll be ready for whatever they throw at us."

The players, though initially disheartened, channeled their disappointment into determination.
The buzzing anticipation in the gymnasium was met with Coach Ethan's commanding yet reassuring presence.

"Alright team" Ethan started. " Our next challenge is the Rebels and the formidable duo of the Twins, so listen up, because here's our plan for the game!" He finished with a determined tone in his voice.

1. Double-Team and Trap:
Coach Ethan initiated the plan by addressing the defensive approach. "Whenever either twin gets the ball, we double-team and trap. Make them uncomfortable, disrupt their passing options and force turnovers. Remember, coordination is key."

In practice drills, the Waves fine-tuned their defensive synchronization. Riley's agility became a weapon in trapping situations, while Jordan's defensive prowess added an extra layer of complexity for the Twins.

2. Rebounding Pressure:
Understanding the Twins' penchant for fast breaks, Coach Ethan shifted the focus to rebounding. "We need to pressure their rebounder, disrupt their outlet passes, and limit their transition game. Every board we secure is a step towards controlling the pace."

Drills centered on disrupting outlet passes showcased the team's collective effort. Jess, with her height advantage, became a pivotal figure in limiting second-chance opportunities, adding a layer of complexity to the Twins' offensive strategies.

3. Strategic Offensive Movement:
Transitioning to offensive strategies, Coach Ethan emphasized, "Moving the ball is our strength. Reverse the ball, exploit gaps left by the twins' defensive rotations, and attack where they aren't. Make them work on both ends of the floor."

Players engaged in drills highlighting fluid ball movement and strategic positioning. Maya and Alex, recognizing offensive opportunities, showcased their ability to exploit gaps created by the Twins' defensive rotations.

4. Communication:
"Effective communication is non-negotiable," Coach Ethan declared. "Vocal leadership on the court ensures seamless coordination. Call out switches, alert teammates, and trust each other to cover defensive assignments."

Drills were designed to enhance on-court communication, with players taking charge in guiding each other through defensive switches and offensive plays. Riley and Jordan, as leaders on the court, as well as Alex, the defensive specialist, set the tone for vocal coordination.

As the team prepared for the Semi-Final clash against the Rebels, there was an unspoken understanding that this encounter held the weight of their previous battles. The stakes were high, the atmosphere charged with determination, and the Waves were poised to write a new chapter in their rivalry against the Rebels.

In a welcome break from the intense lead-up to the showdown with the Rebels, Riley, Jordan, Alex, and Maya headed to the local gym, united in their support for Jess in the Local League Grand Final. The Surfside Sharks, Jess's team, had made a surprise run to the grand final, and the presence of her Waves teammates added an undeniable spark to her spirit.

On the court, Jess was a revelation, her every move resonating with determination and skill. She commanded the paint, her rebounds and blocks a testament to her relentless drive. With each point she scored, the gym pulsed with the rhythm of a team rising together.

"Yeah, Jess!" Alex screamed with excitement from the sidelines after another 2 points from Jess.

"Let's go" yelled Riley and Jordan in unison.

As the game concluded and the Surfside Sharks emerged victorious, the atmosphere was electric. Jess, surrounded by her teammates, shone with the glow of a champion. Riley, Jordan, Maya, and Alex watched on, their cheers mingling with the crowd's jubilation.

Walking away from the gym that night, the team felt a renewed sense of camaraderie. It wasn't just about the victories or the losses; it was about the unspoken vows of support, the shared smiles, and the silent promises to always show up for one another, no matter the court or the challenge ahead.

After the celebrations from Jess' Local League grand final win, soon enough it was game day for the Waves.

As the girls arrived at the stadium they chatted and tried to keep the mood light, hiding their obvious nerves of the upcoming game.

"Make sure you bring those moves from the Grand Final Jess," joked Riley, her tone half humor half serious.

In the warm-ups, the team looked focused, ready for the challenge that lay ahead. With only a minute left before tip-off Coach Ethan gathered the Waves, his words carrying a blend of encouragement and tactical focus.

"Listen up, team. This is it, the moment we've been working for. I've seen your dedication, your growth, and your relentless spirit on the court. Today's game is different, a formidable challenge, but remember, you've got the skills, the strategy, and each other."

His eyes met each player's gaze, emphasizing the unity that defined their journey.

"Remember our plan for taming the twins. Double-team and trap when they get the ball. Put pressure on their rebounder to limit their fast breaks. Move the ball quickly on offense, attack when the twins are rotating, and make them play. We can do this! Trust in your training, trust in each other, and leave everything on the court. Go get them!"

"Bring it in, girls!" Alex called out, her voice brimming with enthusiasm.

"Waves on three," she announced. The team huddled closer, their voices unified as they counted down together. "1, 2, 3, Waves!"

The plan was set, and the strategy clear. Now, it was time to execute on the court and seize the opportunity that awaited them.

A cheer went up from both teams' excited crowds as the referee walked to the center of the court. As the whistle echoed through the pulsating court, the plan was set, and players ready.

"Game on" Riley whispered to herself.
The game began with a flurry of intense play and nervous shots. But the Waves were prepared!

In a double-team and trap scenario, Riley and Jordan moved in unison, converging on one of the twins as she received the ball. The pressure mounted, disrupting passing options and forcing a turnover. Maya, sensing the opportunity, snatched the loose ball and initiated a swift counterattack.

Executing the strategic offensive movement, the Waves moved the ball with precision. Riley, with a calculated dribble, drew the defense towards her. Seizing the moment, she unleashed a bullet pass to Alex, positioned strategically to exploit the gap left by the twins' rotations. Alex, cool and composed, sank a mid-range jump shot.

The rebounding pressure strategy came to life as Jess, with her commanding presence, dominated the boards. The Twins denied the chance to ignite their lethal fast break, struggled to establish their transition game.

However, amidst the strategic brilliance, a subplot unfolded. Jordan, fuelled by a burning desire to succeed, found herself entangled in frustration. Attempting to do too much, she struggled to find her rhythm. Coach Ethan, observing her plight, subbed her out to provide guidance and let her calm down.

"Jordan, trust the plan. Trust your teammates. You've got the talent; let the game come to you," Coach Ethan advised.

As Ethan walked away re-focussing on the game, Jordan fuming with frustration slammed the bench in anger at the unfolding events.

"Enough!" Ethan snapped, momentarily losing his composure "Now is not the time. We've got a game to win"

As Jordan took a moment on the sideline, the Rebels seized the opportunity, surging ahead and taking a lead in the game. The Twins, Emily and Olivia, turned the game into a display of their uncanny synergy. With precise, almost telepathic passes and coordinated movements, they sliced through the Waves' defense.

Coach Ethan glanced at Jordan, understanding the fire within her.
"Let me know when you're ready to go back in," he said.

Emily, with her keen eye and swift decisions, orchestrated the plays, finding Olivia in the perfect spots. Olivia, her movements fluid and decisive, maneuvered around defenders, her layups and mid-range shots finding their mark with frustrating regularity. Their seamless collaboration bewildered the Waves, leaving little room for retaliation.
The Rebels' offense revolved around the Twins' rhythm, their understanding of each other's game elevating the entire team's performance. With each successful play, the Rebels' confidence soared, their

lead widening as the Waves struggled to find their footing without Jordan's stabilizing presence on the court.

Searching for answers, Ethan glanced down the bench his eyes meeting Jordan's.
"You ready?" he questioned.

She replied with determination in her voice, "I'm ready."

Substituted back in, Jordan transformed the game. Her explosive moves and precision shots
fuelled The Waves, as they launched a swift counterattack.

In a seamless exchange, Jordan executed a pick-and-roll with Riley. Like a well-practiced symphony, Riley's dribble drew defenders, and Jordan, with a burst of speed, maneuvered into an open space. Riley's precise pass found Jordan, who rose for a mid-range jumper. The ball sailed through the air, swishing through the net with satisfying precision.

Coach Ethan, on the sideline, clapped in approval. "That's the way, Jordan! Trust in your game, and let the plays unfold."
As the Rebels attempted to regain control, Maya intercepted a pass with lightning reflexes. With a quick outlet to Jordan, the Waves initiated a fast break. Jordan, showcasing her athleticism, drove to

the basket with determination. The defenders caught off guard, attempted to block her path, but Jordan skillfully sidestepped, finishing with a graceful layup.

The crowd roared with excitement as the Waves closed the gap. The game intensified, each possession critical. The strategic brilliance of Coach Ethan's game plan unfolded on the court. Jordan, now in sync with her teammates, set up a series of plays that showcased the Waves seamless coordination.

With seconds ticking away, Riley and Jordan executed a two-player game that left the Twin's defense scrambling. Riley, with a deceptive dribble, drew attention, creating a sliver of space for Jordan. The pass was quick and precise, and Jordan, with a swift release, made the layup.

"Unbelievable!" What a comeback!" exclaimed voices from the crowd as the Waves tied the game with a spectacular play.

Coach Ethan, a beacon of calm on the sideline, offered a nod of approval. "Great teamwork, girls. One more defensive stand, and we've got this."

As the final seconds unfolded, the Waves, fuelled by teamwork and determination, put a hard trap on and denied the Rebels any good scoring opportunities. Olivia, one of the Rebels twins, hurled a shot up as the buzzer sounded, but the shot never looked like going in. With the scores still tied, the game was heading to overtime!

In the huddle, Coach Ethan rallied his team. "We've got extra time, but stick to the plan. Tame those twins, execute our plays, and let's win this game!" The Waves, their spirits high after the thrilling comeback took a collective breath and prepared for the challenge to come.

Overtime unfurled like a high-stakes drama, the tension palpable in every moment. The Twins, Olivia, and Emily, with their skill and agility, orchestrated plays that seemed destined to secure victory. Each time, Riley and Jordan responded with equal fervor, refusing to yield to the mounting pressure.

With seconds ticking away, the Rebels gained a slim 1 point lead, their fans roaring in anticipation of a triumphant finish. After a missed Waves shot, the Twins executed a fast break, weaving through defenders with a fluidity that left the Waves momentarily on the back foot. A collective gasp echoed through the arena as a pass left the fingertips of one of the Twins, seemingly destined for her equally talented sister and the game-winning basket.
But then, like a lightning bolt, Riley intercepted the pass! With quick thinking, she initiated a counterattack, dribbling past defenders and finding an opening. Riley with only seconds left, pulled up over the defenders and released a high-arching floater

destined for the ring. As the ball sailed through the air before bouncing off the back of the rim and back into play, Jordan, with impeccable timing, leaped for an aggressive rebound. The gym echoed with the thud of the ball in her hands.

With the seconds dwindling, Jordan, under immense pressure, spotted Riley in the clear. She delivered a precise pass, threading through two defenders. Riley, with nerves of steel, caught the ball. The Rebels, desperate to prevent a game-winning shot, fouled Riley as she tried to shoot just as the final buzzer sounded.

The gym fell into a hush as Riley stood on the free-throw line with the Bayside Waves still trailing by 1 point. The weight of the moment hung heavy in the air. Two shots, one chance to win, one chance to rewrite history.

The referee signaled for the first shot. Riley, with focus etched on her face, took a deep breath. "Just like shooting at home," she thought to herself as every eye in the stadium focussed on her.
The ball left her hands, gracefully arcing through the air, and swished through the net. The crowd erupted into cheers.

Tie Game!

The gym fell into a haunting silence as Riley prepared for the decisive second shot. The atmosphere was electric, anticipation hanging in the air like a charged storm. Riley, unyielding under the spotlight, following her familiar routine, released the ball. Time seemed to stand still as it traced a perfect trajectory, finding its mark once again. As the ball swished through the net, the crowd went wild. Riley, with nerves of steel, had made both shots to win the game!

The ball had hardly hit the ground before the Waves rushed Riley in celebration. They'd done it! They had beaten the Rebels and now were only one win away from being crowned Champions!

In the euphoria of victory, Coach Ethan gathered the team for a post-game talk, his voice a steady anchor amid the jubilation.

"Fantastic job, girls! That was a hard-fought battle, and you've earned every bit of this victory. Celebrate tonight, enjoy the moment, but remember, our journey isn't over yet," Coach Ethan asserted, a twinkle of pride in his eyes.

The players, their adrenaline still pumping, exchanged smiles, high-fives, and hugs. Riley and Jordan shared a look of mutual accomplishment.

Coach Ethan continued, "We've got a Grand Final to prepare for in a week's time against the Comets. What matters is that we stay focused, keep honing our skills, and bring the same intensity to the final showdown."

Maya, Alex, and Jess nodded in agreement, absorbing Coach Ethan's words. The taste of victory lingered, but the seasoned coach knew the importance of looking forward.

"Enjoy this win, but come next practice, we shift our focus to the Grand Final. Every pass, every shot, and every defensive play counts. We're in this together, Waves, and we're chasing greatness," Coach Ethan declared, instilling a renewed sense of purpose.

As the team dispersed, the gym echoed with laughter and shared triumph. The path to the Grand Final lay ahead, and the Waves, fuelled by their recent victory, were ready to embrace the challenge that awaited them.

In the quiet aftermath of the celebratory chaos, Jordan approached Coach Ethan, a hint of introspection in her eyes. The coach, keenly perceptive, welcomed her with a knowing smile.

"Coach, I want to talk about what happened in the game," Jordan began, her voice a mix of sincerity, embarrassment, and self-reflection.

Coach Ethan, with a reassuring nod, gestured for her to continue.

"I got caught up in trying to do too much, and I could feel it affecting the team. I let frustration take over," Jordan confessed, her gaze focused on the floor.

Coach Ethan, placing a supportive hand on her shoulder, acknowledged, "It happens to the best of us, Jordan. Basketball is a game of passion and emotion. What matters is how you responded."

Jordan looked up, meeting Coach Ethan's gaze, "I appreciate you subbing me out. It helped me collect myself and come back with a clear mind."

The coach smiled, "You showed resilience, Jordan. It's not about avoiding frustration but learning to channel it positively. In the end, you came back in and made a significant impact. That's the mark of a truly great player."

"Now, next week, we've got a Grand Final to win!"

Jordan nodded, a sense of pride mingling with gratitude. The quiet conversation held a valuable lesson — the ability to overcome personal struggles for the greater good of the team. As they exchanged a final nod, the two left the stadium, ready for the challenge of what the Grand Final would bring.

CHAPTER 20:

FOR ALL THE CHOCOLATES

The week leading up to the Grand Final was a whirlwind of anticipation and nerves. The Waves were determined, their sights set on the championship.

In the waning light most afternoons, Riley's backyard transformed into her personal training ground. With her textbooks temporarily forgotten on the kitchen table, she focused solely on perfecting her moves. Each dribble and shot was a step closer to her dream, the rhythm of the ball against the concrete a steady beat marking her dedication. The grand final loomed large in her mind, each practice shot fuelled by the blend of nerves and excitement that only such a game could bring.

Across town, Jordan was in her own world of preparation. Her driveway echoed with the sound of her consistent jump shots, the net swishing in agreement with her precision. She moved with a purpose, visualizing the court, her opponents, and the plays that would soon unfold. Her determination was as clear as the focused look in her eyes, a silent promise to bring her best to the game that mattered most.

Meanwhile, Alex was huddled over her laptop, her room lit by the soft glow of the screen. Videos of the Comets' previous games played, her keen eyes catching every detail, every play. She took notes, her mind weaving strategies, dissecting their patterns, and crafting counterplays. Her dedication to understanding the game was as much a part of her as her tenacious defense on the court.

Maya, putting her Soccer ball aside for the week, practiced her signature shots. The arc of the ball against the sky was a familiar sight, each successful three-pointer a testament to her hard work and innate talent. She knew the importance of her role, the need for her accuracy from the perimeter, and she honed her skill with a single-minded focus.

In the solitude of her home gym, Jess was a force of nature. The timing of her jumps, the precision of her blocks and rebounds, were practiced with a relentless intensity. Each leap was higher, each movement more fluid, a dance of strength and grace that spoke of her commitment and the role she would play in the team's success.

Each girl, in her own space, was united by a common goal. The grand final was not just a game; it was the culmination of every drop of sweat, every moment of practice, and every shared dream. And as the day of the grand final approached, they were ready – not just as players, but as a team, a unit forged in dedication and bound by a single aim: victory.

Coach Ethan, aware of the formidable opponent in Gemma and the Comets, spent hours rewatching their previous games against the Comets looking for ways to control Gemma's impact on the game.
Looking over all of his notes, Ethan devised a plan aimed at neutralizing her impact.

The final training session of the season held a mix of intensity and nostalgia under the bright lights of the Waves home court. Coach Ethan gathered his team, his gaze sweeping over the young athletes he'd guided through countless drills and games. The air was charged with a silent understanding; this was more than just a practice—it was the culmination of a season's worth of growth, challenges, and triumphs.

"Team," Ethan began, his voice steady and sure, "this season has been an incredible journey. Each one of you has pushed beyond your limits, and grown not just as players but as individuals. I couldn't be prouder of the hard work and heart you've all shown."

The team listened, the bond they shared with their coach evident in their attentive silence. Ethan had been more than a coach; he'd been a mentor, a supporter, and a crucial part of their basketball journey.

"But our work isn't done yet," Ethan continued, shifting the focus to the upcoming grand final. "We're up against a tough team, and we all know the kind of threat Gemma poses." He paused, ensuring he had their full attention. "Our game plan needs to be precise, focused and executed flawlessly. We stop Gemma, we disrupt their rhythm, we win the game."

"This is the Stopping Gemma Plan" he started. "Yes I know it could've had a better name" he finished as the team began to laugh, momentarily breaking the intensity of the moment.

He laid out the strategy, a meticulous blueprint designed to neutralize the Comets' star player.

1. Force her to the baseline:
"Limit Gemma's options. Force her toward the baseline, cut off her angles, and deny easy access to the basket. Make her work for every point." Coach Ethan emphasized.

2. Help from Jess using her height:
Jess, the tall center, would play a crucial role. "Use your height advantage, Jess. Contest her shots, disrupt her vision, and be a defensive wall in the paint."

3. Deny the return pass:
Once Gemma passed the ball, the Waves would tighten their defense. "Don't let her become a playmaker. Deny her the return pass, force turnovers, and capitalize on fast breaks."

The team nodded, each member mentally preparing to play their part in the strategy. Ethan's words weren't just instructions; they were the final pieces of a season-long puzzle, a testament to their growth and their shared ambition to end the season as champions.

"As we step onto that court," Ethan concluded, "remember, it's not just about the plays we run or the points we score. It's about showing the heart and unity that's defined us all season. Let's bring this home, Waves."

With that, the team broke into their last practice, each pass, each shot, and each drill a step towards their final goal.

●

The night before the game, Riley and Jordan shared quiet moments readying themselves for the challenge ahead. Lying awake, Riley replayed moments from previous games in her mind, while Jordan, her basketball in hand, whispered affirmations of strength and determination.

The day of the grand final unfurled with a blend of routine and restless anticipation. At their schools, Riley and Jordan navigated their classes with a distant focus, their minds inevitably drifting toward the evening's game.

As the final bell rang, signifying the end of the school day, the usual chatter and laughter of students were overshadowed by an uncharacteristic quietness that enveloped Riley and Jordan. They were islands of calm in a sea of after-school energy, their thoughts singularly honed in on the impending game. The journey home was a time of reflection and mental preparation, a moment to transition from students to athletes.

The drive to the arena was a journey charged with contemplation and silent resolve. Riley and Jordan's parents didn't even bother to try and lighten the mood and chat during the drive there. They knew their daughters. They knew they were focused, ready.

As the cityscape gave way to the illuminated facade of the arena, the significance of the moment settled in. Here, under the bright lights and expectant gazes, their season's journey would find its thrilling end.

Arriving at the gymnasium, the shift in atmosphere was immediate. The tranquil introspection of the day gave way to a palpable buzz of excitement. The gym, now a beacon of anticipation, welcomed them with the familiar scent of polished wood and the resonant sound of basketballs echoing off the walls. Here, in this sacred space of competition, all the day's subdued energy was channeled into a singular purpose – to rise to the challenge of the grand final, a test of skill, teamwork, and the culmination of a season's worth of dedication and dreams.

The gymnasium was buzzing with an electric energy, palpable and vibrant, as fans filled the stands for the much-anticipated grand final. Bright lights illuminated the court, casting a glow on the players as they went through their final warm-up routines. The tension and excitement in the air were almost tangible, a mixture of nervous anticipation and the thrill of the impending high-stakes game.

The court announcer's voice boomed through the speakers, cutting through the hum of the crowd. "Ladies and gentlemen, welcome to the grand finale of this season's basketball championship!" The crowd erupted in cheers, a wave of applause and shouts rolling through the stands. "Introducing first, the Kingstown Comets," the announcer continued, his voice rising over the buzzing stadium. One by one, the names of the opposing team's players were called out. Each player jogged onto the court to the sound of their name, acknowledging the crowd with waves or nods, their faces a mix of focus and determination. Gemma, the team's star player was announced last. Walking calmly to join her teammates, a look of determined focus written all over her face, the Waves knew they were in for a challenge.

Then came the moment for the Bayside Waves. "And now, please welcome the Bayside Waves!" The crowd's response was deafening, a thunderous roar of support that filled the gym. The announcer's voice rang out, announcing each player. "Starting with the dynamic guard, Riley..." she sprinted onto the court, her eyes blazing with intensity. "At forward, the relentless Jordan..." She followed, her expression steely and resolute. The introductions continued, with Alex, Maya, Jess, and the rest of the team each taking their turn in the spotlight, their names greeted with enthusiastic cheers. As they lined up, facing their opponents, the atmosphere was charged with an almost surreal sense of anticipation. This was more than a game; it was a culmination of their hard work, dreams, and aspirations.

The atmosphere in the stadium was electric as the Grand Final tipped off. The Comets and the Waves locked horns in a fierce battle for supremacy. The Waves, however, struggled to find their rhythm. Shots that usually found the mark now bounced off the rim, and passes that flowed seamlessly were intercepted.

Gemma on the other hand, was dominating the game. She was creating plays for her teammates, attacking the middle at every opportunity making the defence collapse, and creating gaps behind the Waves for easy baskets for the Comets.

The usual flare and offense prowess of Riley and Jordan was also off. Swift passes lead to fumbled catches, miss-timed shots lead to Comets rebounds and easy transition points.

Ethan, sensing the urgency, called a timeout. "We're flat, but we've got one more gear. Let's switch to a full-court press. We need to disrupt their flow and spark our offense. Everyone, bring the intensity!"

The Waves though, found little success with the press. The Comets, led by Gemma, showcased exceptional ball-handling and composure. The gap widened, and the dream of a championship slipped further away.

As the game progressed, Gemma and the Comets, maintained their relentless offensive onslaught. The Waves, despite their defensive efforts, struggled to contain Gemma's scoring prowess. The plan to force her to the baseline faced stiff resistance as Gemma showcased her versatility by connecting from various angles on the court.

Riley, usually a beacon of offensive brilliance, found herself tightly marked by the Comets' defenders leaving her unable to get her usual game going. Even her favorite behind the back dribble and drive move was ineffective. Gemma's defensive pressure disrupted the Waves usual fluid ball movement, and their attempts to reverse the play were met with quick defensive rotations.

Alex, the defensive specialist, battled admirably against Gemma, attempting to deny her the return pass. However, the Comets' ball movement and Gemma's court awareness created openings, and the Waves faced a constant challenge in disrupting their plays.

The gap widened despite Coach Ethan's strategic adjustments. Maya, the sharpshooter, struggled to find her rhythm, and the Comets capitalized on turnovers, converting them into fast breaks. Jess, while contesting shots in the paint, faced difficulty in slowing down Gemma's scoring spree.

In the closing moments, the full-court press initially intended to spark a comeback, proved ineffective against the composed Comets. The final buzzer echoed through the stadium, signaling the end of the Grand Final and the Waves' season. The scoreboard may have read a Waves loss, however, it told a story of determination, effort, and a dream left unfulfilled.

As the Waves watched the Comets celebrate their Grand Final victory and walked off the court, a mix of emotions filled the air. Disappointment hung heavy. The feeling of pride in a journey filled with growth and friendship was not able to be felt this soon after the devastation of losing the most important game. Coach Ethan, despite the loss, approached each player, offering words of encouragement and gratitude for their relentless effort.

"Remember this moment, team," Coach Ethan said, gathering the players. "Championships may elude us today, but the resilience you've shown defines true victory. Don't let one disappointing game ruin what was a great season. We'll come back stronger, learn from this, and embrace the challenges ahead. This season might be finished, but our journey continues."

While Ethan's words were encouraging to his team, he knew that the night's game was a missed opportunity. In the semifinal, the team was an unstoppable force, their synergy on the court akin to a well-conducted orchestra. Each player hit their cues perfectly, their movements fluid and confident, as if each dribble, pass, and shot were destined to succeed. The game felt less like a contest and more like a declaration, a testament to their hard work and unyielding dedication throughout the season. It was a performance that seemed touched by magic, each moment a brushstroke in a masterpiece of athletic prowess.

But in the grand final, that same magic seemed elusive, as if the spell that had carried them had wavered. The fluidity that defined their semifinal victory was replaced by a hesitancy, the confident strides now cautious steps. It wasn't for lack of effort or desire; the fire that drove them was as fierce as ever. Yet, the synchronicity that once felt instinctual now seemed a beat out of time. Passes didn't find their mark with the usual precision, shots that once felt guided by an unseen hand now bounced away from the rim, and the defense that had been impenetrable showed cracks under the pressure.

It was as if the team was chasing the ghost of their semifinal selves, trying to recapture a form that, for reasons beyond their grasp, slipped through their fingers when they needed it most. The grand final wasn't just a game; it was a lesson in the temporary nature of perfection. It taught that even the most flawless performance one day could be an elusive mirage the next, reminding everyone that in sports, as in life, the magic isn't in a single victory but in the journey, the trials, and the relentless pursuit of excellence.

In the aftermath of the final buzzer, the atmosphere in the gymnasium shifted from electric excitement to a more somber tone as the medal presentation ceremony commenced. The players of the team, their faces a blend of disappointment and pride, lined up to receive their runner-up medals. As each player stepped forward, their name called out into the echoing gym a round of applause rose from the stands. The applause was not just for their performance in the final game, but for their entire season's journey – a testament to their skill, teamwork, and perseverance.

As they draped the silver medals around their necks, the players exchanged glances – some teary-eyed, others wearing forced smiles. The weight of the medals felt bittersweet; each one a symbol of how close they had come to their ultimate goal. Coach gathered them for a final huddle, his words echoing both encouragement and consolation. "This isn't the end, but a beginning," he said, his voice steady and reassuring. "You've shown yourselves to be champions, regardless of the outcome today." In that huddle, amidst the mixed emotions, there was a palpable sense of unity and resolve – a silent vow that they would return stronger, turning the pain of today's loss into motivation for the future.

Jordan, visibly disheartened, approached Coach Ethan. "I wanted this so badly, Coach. I feel like I let the team down."

Ethan placed a reassuring hand on her shoulder. "You gave it your all, Jordan. The journey doesn't end here. This is just the beginning. Remember the lessons, savor the victories, and let the defeats fuel your hunger for the next challenge."

After the presentations the Waves left the court, heads held high, knowing that in basketball and life, every setback was a setup for a comeback.

CHAPTER 21:

A NEW HORIZON

In the wake of the grand final, the weeks seemed to blend together for Riley and Jordan. Their conversations, once filled with the excitement of the season, now often circled back to the what-ifs of the final game. Despite the disappointment, they found solace in their shared determination for the upcoming tryouts, practicing relentlessly, their eyes set on the new season.

The new season of the girls local games had started and served as a timely distraction from the disappointment of the grand final.

Under the glow of stadium lights, Riley and Jordan found themselves on the familiar courts where their journey began. Watching younger age groups games while waiting for their own the two girls rhythmic took a moment to absorb the season that had just unfolded.

"I hate that we lost," Jordan admitted, her eyes fixed on the action on the court ahead of them. "It burns, you know?"

Riley nodded, sharing the sentiment. "I've been practicing at home every day reliving all the moments that went against us. Wishing I could go back and play differently"

Jordan gritted her teeth, and shook her head in frustration. Still dwelling on the events of the grand final and replaying every moment in their minds, a familiar figure caught their attention as he approached. The reassuring presence of Coach Ethan calmed the minds of the two girls.

The low key high five from Ethan to both Riley and Jordan was a regular welcome between the trio.

"Still hurting, huh?" questioned Ethan.

"Don't worry, I am too" he continued. "I keep thinking about all the little moments that we could've done differently"

In moments like these, it was easy to see why the three of them got on so well. Each of them as competitive as the other.

Ethan didn't need to wait for the girls responses, the unspoken bond that had been created throughout the season left him knowing the girls were thinking the same.

"So! we heard you'll be coaching against us in the local comp," Jordan said, a mix of surprise and excitement in her voice.

Ethan nodded, "That's right. It's a new challenge for all of us. But remember, no matter which side of the court we're on, I'll always have your back!"

"Just don't expect any special treatment, when we play against you, and my team starts whipping you guys on court" Ethan said with a confident smirk.

Both girls laughed! "Yeah Right" exclaimed Jordan.

"Good luck with that!" Riley quickly chimed in.

"I'll have something for you, just you wait" Ethan replied laughing.

"So, tryouts this weekend," Riley said, her gaze again, fixed on the court. "What if we end up on different teams?"

Jordan chuckled, "As if!"

"Ready for the tryouts?" Ethan asked, his gaze reflecting pride.

"Absolutely," Riley replied.

Jordan added, "Bring it"

As the conversation drew to a close, Coach Ethan stood, gathering his coaching bag. The shift from their coach to coaching the Blues in the local league was a change, but one he looked forward to with enthusiasm. "Alright, I've got to get going. The Blues need their coach," he said with a grin, referencing his new team.

Riley couldn't resist the opportunity for a playful jab, her eyes sparkling with mischief. "Make sure you don't teach them too well, Coach. We wouldn't want to lose to you in the local league," she teased, her tone light but competitive.

Jordan chimed in, matching Riley's playful tone. "Yeah, remember, if you start winning too much, we might have to come and show the Blues how it's really done," she added, a mock-serious look on her face.

Ethan laughed, appreciating their banter. "I'd like to see you try," he retorted with a smile. "Just keep playing the way you are, and I'll have to keep finding new strategies to beat you both."

With a final wave, Coach Ethan headed out, leaving Riley and Jordan laughing in his wake. Their relationship with Ethan was built on mutual respect, a dynamic that extended beyond the court. As Ethan walked away, Riley and Jordan started to prepare for their own games. They pulled their new shoes out of their bags, laced them up, and headed to their respective courts.

"Good luck, loser," Jordan quipped sarcastically.

Without even turning around, Riley threw out a peace sign with her hand, replied, "See you at tryouts," then disappeared around the corner, ready for her game.

The weekend arrived quickly, and the pre-tryouts anticipation buzzed throughout both new and existing players. The many girls on court awaited the arrival of the coaches and the beginning of the tryouts for the new season.

Soon enough, the coaches, lead by the excited, yet focussed and determined Ethan gathered the players mid court. Riley and Jordan, this time standing side by side, looked through the crowd seeing some old faces, but also some new girls they hadn't seen before. Upon catching the eyes of Alex and Jess, exchanged a subtle nod in recognition of the past season and a silent promise, an unspoken contract of doing everything they could to go one better in the upcoming season.

The players listened intently to Ethans words and advice about the upcoming tryout and season and were keen to showcase their basketball talents to the coaches.

And so, as Ethan lined all the players up for their first drill of the tryouts Riley and Jordan were eager to leave the disappointment of the grand final loss behind them.

Waiting for their drill to start, and as always nowadays, side by side, Ethan stood next to his star dynamic duo. Riley and Jordan both looked up at him eagerly as he simply questioned with a smile...

"You ready?"

Riley and Jordan will return.

Explore the Game Time Tales Series Further

For additional insights into the Game Time Tales Series and to access comprehensive resources tailored for parents about our books, we invite you to scan the code provided below. Look for the 'Players Page' for detailed information about the series, enriching your understanding and engagement with our collection.

Made in United States
North Haven, CT
24 May 2025

69173027R00078